It's easy to follow the crowd and to do things the "common" way. Susie Larson's call to take the higher road, live life God's way, and be an "uncommon" woman is a refreshing message we desperately need to hear. You won't just read this book . . . you'll be inspired to live it out every day!

> Jill Savage
> Founder and Executive Director of Hearts at Home
> Author of *My Hearts at Home*

Who wants to be a "common" woman? Not me, and I'm guessing you don't want to be one either. Let Susie Larson guide you through the Word of God, learning from Him how we can be the women He has called us to be . . . resilient, wise, forgiving, loving . . . God has written the instructions. Susie is here to help us apply them. The result? An uncommon woman!

> Kendra Smiley
> Conference speaker and author of *Do Your Kids a Favor:*
> *Love Your Spouse* (with John Smiley)

Susie Larson gently leads women into an extraordinary life through perceptive and personal insights and a challenge to live beyond our feelings or circumstances, but also to experience the freedom and joy of living an uncommon life. This is a book that is not just a good read—it's life changing.

> T. Suzanne Eller
> Author of *The Woman I Am Becoming: Embrace the Chase*
> *for Identity, Faith, and Destiny*

Oh, how I want to be the kind of uncommon woman Susie Larson writes about so poetically! Her winsome, hard-won message beckons me toward the all-consuming embrace of Jesus, away from my petty need for approval. If every woman dared to pick up *The Uncommon Woman* and live the kind of extraordinary life Susie thrusts her way, the world would be turned upside down.

> Mary E. DeMuth
> Author of *Ordinary Mom, Extraordinary God,*
> *Watching the Tree Limbs*

Susie Larson's *The Uncommon Woman* is for *every* woman. With a real heart for Jesus and her Christian sisters, Susie shows us how to lean on the Lord during the different seasons of our lives. Susie Larson is a great writer for our time . . . a difficult time such as this that we live in.

Susan Wales
Author and Producer

the

uncommon
woman

making an
ordinary life
extraordinary

susie larson

MOODY PUBLISHERS
CHICAGO

All Scripture quotations, unless otherwise indicated, are taken from the *Holy Bible, New International Version*®. NIV®. Copyright © 1973, 1978, 1984 by International Bible Society. Used by permission of Zondervan. All rights reserved.

Scripture quotations marked NLT are taken from the *Holy Bible, New Living Translation*, copyright © 1996, 2004. Used by permission of Tyndale House Publishers, Inc., Wheaton Illinois 60189, U.S.A. All rights reserved.

Scripture quotations marked THE MESSAGE are from *The Message*, copyright © by Eugene H. Peterson 1993, 1994, 1995. Used by permission of NavPress Publishing Group.

Scripture quotations marked AMP are taken from *The Amplified Bible*. Copyright © 1965, 1987 by The Zondervan Corporation. *The Amplified New Testament* copyright © 1958, 1987 by The Lockman Foundation. Used by permission.

Scripture quotations marked GNT are from the Good News Translation in Today's English Version—Second Edition Copyright © 1992 by American Bible Society. Used by Permission.

Scripture quotations marked TNIV are taken from the *Holy Bible, Today's New International Version* TNIV®. Copyright© 2001, 2005 by International Bible Society. Used by permission of Zondervan. All rights reserved.

Scriptures quotations marked NCV are from the *Holy Bible, New Century Version*, copyright © 1987, 1988, 1991 by Word Publishing, Nashville, TN 37214. Used by permission.

Scripture quotations marked NKJV are taken from the *New King James Version*. Copyright © 1982 by Thomas Nelson, Inc. Used by permission. All rights reserved.

Emphasis was added to Scripture by the author.

Published in association with the literary agency of Alive Communications, Inc., 7680 Goddard Street, Suite 200, Colorado Springs, CO 80920, www.alivecommunications.com <http://www.alivecommunications.com/>.

Editor: Pam Pugh
Interior Design: Ragont Design
Cover Design: The Terry Dugan Design Group
Cover Image: Manuel Ribeiro, iStockphoto.com (image #4876550)

Library of Congress Cataloging-in-Publication Data

Larson, Susie, 1962-
    The uncommon woman : making an ordinary life extraordinary / by Susie Larson.
        p. cm.
    Includes bibliographical references.
    ISBN 978-0-8024-5279-5
    1. Christian women--Religious life. 2. Christian life. I. Title.

    BV4527.L375 2008
    248.8'43--dc22

                                                                        2008007039

ISBN-10: 0-8024-5279-5

We hope you enjoy this book from Moody Publishers. Our goal is to provide high-quality, thought-provoking books and products that connect truth to your real needs and challenges. For more information on other books and products written and produced from a biblical perspective, go to www.moodypublishers.com or write to:

Moody Publishers
820 N. LaSalle Boulevard
Chicago, IL 60610

3 5 7 9 10 8 6 4 2

Printed in the United States of America

This book is lovingly dedicated to:

My Golden Girls
Uncommon Women, All of Them

Bonnie Newberg, Janet Nelson, Susan Stuart, and Diane Stores

These older, wiser mentors have ministered incredible
life and wisdom into my soul.
Because of you, dear friends, I am forever changed.

And to:

My Beloved Husband, Kevin

Honey, I couldn't do this without you
I love you so much

And to:

My Sweet Jesus

You show me every day what it means to be Yours
I love You most

Contents

acknowledgments

My deepest thanks go to my amazing publisher, Moody Publishers. You have wrapped your arms around my ministry, my convictions, and me. You have strengthened my message and increased its impact. You have become family to me, and I regularly thank God for you. Blessings to you all.

To my acquisitions editor, Jennifer Lyell
You are a globally minded Kingdom woman, and I appreciate you so very much. Thank you for being much more than an editor. You are a sister and a friend.

To my publicist, Janis Backing
You continually amaze me. Your business savvy, your kindness, and your love for Jesus have blessed me so and made this journey a sweet one. Thanks for all you do.

To my editor, Pam Pugh
You make me laugh, you make me look good, and you challenge me to be better writer. With all my heart, I thank you.

To my amazing literary agent, Beth Jusino

Thank you for taking the time to know me like you do. Bless you for helping me to stay true to the words God gives to me. You are a treasure.

To my parents, Pat and Ed Erickson, whose support I cherish. I love you, Mom and Dad.

To my sample readers

Daryl Jackson, Tootsie Telle, Carrie Kuiken, Cindy Larson, Kay Blake, Karen Telle, Bonnie Newberg, Janet Nelson, Susan Stuart, Judy Chesla, Renee Volk, Shari Carlson, Amy Latter, Julie Hawkinson, Andrea Lupino, Peggy Stoks, Peg Kohler, Patty Fischer, Patty Larson, Linda Mahmarian, Andie Munn, and Amy Larson

To my intercessors who hold me up when I'm writing, speaking, and traveling. This is our fruit and our victory. May you always remember how important you are to me.

I thank God for you.

To my sweet husband, Kevin, and to my precious sons, Jake, Luke, and Jordan

Words fail to express just how much I cherish you all. Boys, when I look at the men you are becoming, my heart swells with gratitude and hope. Our world needs more uncommon men like you. Please press on in His Name.

To Jesus,

Where would I be if not for You?

I praise Your beautiful Name.

before we begin . . .

UNCOMMON: *remarkable, extraordinary, exceptional, singular, significant, special, unearthly, mind-boggling*[1]

My appreciation for the uncommon is still evolving. When I'm knocked down and I get back up again, I admire unrelenting perseverance in others as a virtue worth more than gold. When words get back to me that were meant to injure, I find in my heart a growing longing to walk the righteous road, and to be somebody totally different than the stereotypical woman.

When God burdens my heart with what burdens His, my heroes become those who risk their lives to rescue young girls from brothels, those who put themselves in harm's way for the sake of the gospel, and those who sacrificially give so the hungry can eat and the sick can recover. Their courage and conviction admonish me.

When I dare to ask for the impossible and then I see it come to pass, I find myself amazed by those who *live* by faith. Every. Single. Day. I wonder how much more of an impact I could be making in this world had I more faith.

Deep within our souls is a longing to be an uncommon woman. We are noble creatures with a great capacity for honor, conviction, and compassion. We have within us a strength that can weather storms, a courage that compels us to make a difference, and the living Christ who daily works in us to make us more like Him.

We're all different but the same. We all hurt on occasion. We've thrown the spear and we've been hit a few times. We've said one thing and done another. And we've had our heroic moments when no one else was watching. All of us come to the noble path from a different place. But that doesn't matter so much. Where do we go from here? What do we do with what we now know?

Do you long to rise above the petty behaviors that are familiar to most women? Are you ready for a radical overhaul of how you view yourself, others, and your place in this world? Are you provoked by the pain in the world and do you long to make a difference with this life you've been given?

If yes, then please join me. Let's journey together toward a more dignified existence. Let's look deeply at the truth of who we are and how we view and treat others. Let's get excited about what's possible when we take God at His word. May we together know and embrace our high call as women who belong to the Most High God.

As we shake off the status quo, we will pursue the higher road.

The uncommon woman believes the wonderful truth about herself. Moreover, she has the capacity to view others from this same heavenly perspective. Bursting from her heart is the conviction to do something about the injustices in her world. She walks with a purity that allows her to see God everywhere. And the Kingdom of God is so strong in her life that everywhere she

places her feet suddenly becomes an uncommon and holy place—
because she's there.

You can be that woman. You were meant to be that woman.

*May we live up to our privilege and our responsibility as ones who
belong to Jesus. Let's do this journey together.*

May the Lord Jesus bless you as you read.

@⁀Susie Larson

the uncommon
woman understands
the paradox that
she is nothing
and everything

Uncontaminated trust
in the revelation of Jesus allows
us to breathe more freely, to dance more
joyfully, and to sing more gratefully
about the gift of salvation.[1]

൸Brennan Manning

And so we know and rely on the love
God has for us. God is love. Whoever lives
in love lives in God, and God in him.

൸1 John 4:16

humbly accepts acceptance[2]

My heart was torn in two and ground with gravel from being stepped on, thrown around, and tossed aside. My carpet was wet with tears and I was sprawled facedown on my floor, wondering if the pain would ever go away.

Why was this battle crippling me so? I survived many months on bed rest followed by a devastating disease. I dealt with babies in the hospital, financial brokenness, and my husband's cancer. Those were tough times, but we could endure them because we felt embraced and understood, and we had people to love and support us along the way.

This was a different kind of pain.

I used to walk through life with an underlying sense of insecurity, and it wore like a small sharp rock imbedded in my sandal: impossible to see, but reinjuring me every single day. Even so, the chronic, shooting pain of insecurity had nothing on the agony of the betrayal, rejection, and character assassination I was now enduring.

With everything in me, I cried to the Lord, *"Oh God! This hurts so badly! Help me to see You in this! Show me how to walk through this pain to a better place. I am desperate for You, Lord!"* I felt alone and misunderstood, and the sobs coming from my mouth were deafening my own ears.

Yet all of a sudden, there it was, and my spiritual ears heard it.

I am here for you, My child. You don't have to do this alone. I know rejection. I know the twisting, gripping pain that breaks your heart and makes your skin hurt. I understand it well. But it's time to get up now. I love you. I accept you. And you have things to do in this life. For starters, you are going to pray for your accusers.

Instantly I sat up, wiped my eyes, and looked out the window. The sky was blue and magnificent and the birds seemed happy as ever. I couldn't relate. Using my couch as an altar, I knelt down, folded my hands, and began to pray. I had no love in my heart for my former friends; only anger. I didn't want them blessed; I wanted them squished under the mighty hand of God.

I'm just being honest here.

Even so, I obeyed and I prayed. The more I prayed, the more I realized that this pain—this valley—was lush with fertile soil, ready and waiting for me to plant seeds of faith, forgiveness, and obedience. I realized that before me was a mighty opportunity for growth, miracles, and a fresh revelation of this Man, Jesus.

The Bible says that He prepares a table for me *in the presence* of my enemies. Even if I had to crawl there, I wanted to eat at that table.

                                                      ꩜

What if I could have reclined around *the* table with the disciples and with Jesus—God's Son, the King of the universe—would I have had mixed emotions? I imagine so. On one hand, I'm sure I would have felt tremendous awe and quiet reverence at being so close to the Lord. And yet as I allowed my thoughts to take their natural course, would I also have felt a measure of pride and superiority because I was one of the few who were chosen to hang around and walk with Jesus? Oh, I hope not. But I do wonder.

As the dinner hour approached in the upper room, I imagine the disciples glancing around, looking for the slave who would clean their feet in preparation for the feast. Normally, if no slave was available to do the foot washing, it was customary for one of the guests to volunteer. Since there was no one who seemed ready to subject himself to the task, I wonder if they considered pulling a young servant from the street to do the duty. Perhaps they were murmuring among themselves, wondering out loud how long they would have to wait until dinner was served.

Imagine the jolt they experienced as Jesus got up, tied the servant's towel around His waist, and reached for the basin. Picture them swallowing hard as they awkwardly scooted back to give Him room. As Jesus' hands were dirtied from the filth on their feet, their hearts must have melted and any potential pride had to have been swallowed up and replaced by utter humility.

Even while Jesus was washing their feet, He knew in His heart that *every one of them* would abandon Him at some time that very night.

I have fears, I have insecurities; and had I been with the crowd, I am sure I would have abandoned Him too.

Judas abandoned *and* betrayed Jesus. (Judas wanted power and position, and it had become abundantly clear to him that the man he was following did not share his passion for human influence.) As Jesus rubbed the dirt off of his feet, His heart must have ached deeply, knowing He would be disowned for the price of a slave. Jesus *knew* that these were the feet of the man who would set in motion the most excruciating, agonizing hours of His life. *Still, He served.* Still, He washed, He rubbed, and He lovingly held the feet of the guilty in His hands.

In the days that followed, how many times do you suppose that service was replayed in the disciples' minds? Without question, they had days when they were more cowardly than courageous. Their feet would get dirty again. Jesus knew all of this ahead of time, and He left them with a beautiful memory of His love for them, humbly washing their feet in a way in which they were honored and affirmed. He painted for them an enduring portrait of uncommon and true greatness.

Pondering this exchange between Jesus and the disciples compelled me to face my own dirty feet. The blackened water in the basin was *mine*. Never mind that women had hurt me with their words. It didn't matter that they couldn't stand me. Who had I hurt? Where had I been? And how was I to reconcile my low tendencies and dirty feet with the humility in Christ that took Him lower still?

I didn't have to look too far inside to be completely humbled by my own need for more of Jesus and less of me. But to pray for women who had stones in their hands and their gazes fixed on me seemed almost an impossible feat. To look up to Jesus and ask the question (as Joyce Meyer so eloquently puts it), "What *in me* needed this to happen?" took courage I didn't think I possessed.

From my perspective, their words were like planks while mine felt like slivers. From God's perspective, sin was sin and it's what separates us from Him—and keeps us from seeing clearly. Slivers come from planks and they're all the same, really. They are removed by love and forgiveness. This is ground God and I had covered before; He was just setting the plow a little deeper.

With all my heart I believe that it's not only possible to rise up out of the pain of betrayal and rejection, it's our call, our privilege, and our responsibility as ones who have been redeemed. In fact, I submit that those who tenaciously grab hold of God's promises during such times will rise up and be even more blessed and qualified for His service once the storm subsides. They will have more tenderness in their souls, more compassion and conviction in their actions, and a greater capacity to love and forgive others.

Unfortunately, the *common way* through such times is the road of reciprocating pettiness and gossip, building cases, and forming allegiances. Those who take this path through betrayal and rejection give the devil a mighty foothold in their lives. They emerge from the crisis of betrayal miserable, not blessed. They struggle with suspicion instead of trust. They are more cynical and less hopeful.

To be an uncommon woman is to do what's *un*natural. Like streams in the desert, the uncommon woman has the capacity to find refreshment and *be* a source of refreshment no matter where life finds her.

Here's how I walked through my valleys of rejection and betrayal and came out on the other side with the treasures God had promised me:

> **Step One:** Regularly remind yourself who you are and whose you are in Christ, according to the Word of God (*loved, called, accepted, chosen, cherished, and forgiven*)! Dare to allow the Lord to point out anything in you that might offend Him (see Psalm 139:23–24).

> **Step Two:** Pray for your accusers. Ask God to bless them. This will be tough because you won't want them blessed, but trust me; the more drawn they are to Jesus, the more like Him they'll become.

> **Step Three:** Forgive your accusers. This will be a "hot potato exercise." You will forgive them today—maybe twenty times—then you'll show up tomorrow to forgive them nineteen times. Eventually the potato will stay up in the air, and you will be free to leave the outcome to the Lord.

Step Four: Thank God for everything good in your life. During times of rejection you are at great risk of losing perspective and neglecting those who haven't abandoned or betrayed you.

Step Five: Pray for someone who has it tougher than you do. Write her a note or buy her a gift. Don't lose sight of the fact that even in tough times, God has called you to be a flow-through account of His blessings.

Step Six: Get some exercise. Working your muscles and forcing your blood to circulate will do great things for your body and your mind. Pray while you exercise. Ask the Lord to keep your heart pure.

Step Seven: Get proper rest and then wake up tomorrow morning and begin again with Step One.

꩜

Life gets messy. We make it that way. And yet amidst the dirt that's been thrown at us, the grime on our own feet, and the stones in our hands, we are supposed to believe that we are His treasure. Jesus beckons us off the low road of gossip and insecurity and to a higher place of holy confidence and humble dependence.

He lifts us up out of the ash heap, cleans us off, and teaches us how to sing (see Psalm 40:1–5). He reaches into our lives and, with a surgeon's precision, removes our cancerous character traits while preserving what's beautiful about us. When our spirits are bruised and our wicks are smoldering, He cups His hands around us and breathes life into us again (see Isaiah 42:3; Matthew 12:20). We are everything to Him . . . yet we are nothing without Him.

The uncommon woman understands her capacity for pettiness, selfishness, and a sinful bent that leads her away from the Almighty. But her thoughts don't dwell there. No, despite what she knows about herself, she entrusts herself fully to the One who will shape her into a thing of magnificence.

Accepting acceptance means having the courage to face your foibles without it diminishing your value. Accepting acceptance means refusing to let others define you, because God already has. Accepting acceptance means cherishing the fact that you've been bought with a price, and thus embracing the call to become more and more like Christ every day.

> Jesus knew that the Father had put all things under his power, and that he had come from God and was returning to God; so he got up from the meal, took off his outer clothing, and wrapped a towel around his waist. (John 13:3–4)

To live freely and to embrace acceptance is to walk the way Jesus walked and to believe what He says. He understood *that He came from God and was returning to God*. So He got up from *His place* at the table.

Here lies the key to accepting acceptance. We understand who we are by knowing *whose* we are. First we must embrace this truth—once and for all—that we are a divine creation by a Masterful Artist, and we were made to bring Him glory, to bear much fruit, and to reflect His love.

Do *you* know where you came from and to where you are going? You came from Him! You were God's idea! He knows you best and loves you most because He made you! All of heaven is on your side, which is important because you are called to live a powerful life on earth. When your days are completed and your journey is through, you'll get to see Jesus face-to-face. You'll see firsthand the love in His eyes, and it will make your knees weak! For the briefest moment you'll wish you would have trusted Him more because you'll understand that *nothing* could have separated you from His love.

When we *regularly* identify ourselves as someone Jesus loves
. . . everything changes. When we take that leap of faith to believe
that all we could ever want, need, and hope for is found in Jesus,
life takes on a whole new meaning.

> *Eventually, we are going to believe all the love God has for us. At that
> moment, nothing on earth will be able to stop us from becoming the
> people God has called us to be. Through the leading of the Holy Spirit,
> our confidence and faith in the nature of God can enable us to believe
> fully in the enormity of His love for us.*[3]
>
>   ◊ GRAHAM COOKE

The more we understand that our identity in Christ is *continually* secure and that no misstep, rejection, or judgment could ever
change that, the more liberated we become from the opinions of
others. As the gap increases between God's opinions and others'
opinions, we are able to live more freely and are more consumed
with the idea that heaven is our home and earth is the place to
make Him known.

As we grow in the knowledge of our acceptance in Christ, the
opinions of others will cease to have the power over us they once
had. Not that we become inconsiderate or hardened toward
others; quite the opposite. We *love* people, but we *hope* in God.
We live, breathe, and walk in the *reality* that we are someone God
enjoys, and we look for opportunities to demonstrate His love.

We've embraced acceptance when we are able to step away
from our "place" at the table and get on our knees to serve when
we are called to do so. We become uncommon when we, like
Christ, forgive those who don't deserve it. Quite frankly, we
don't deserve it either. And yet, to walk the high road is to accept
the fact that though we may not *deserve* to be there, we *get* to be
there, because of Him.

We are free when we are able to give without always expecting a thank-you, and serve without always getting the credit. We won't always have to be right, first, or noticed because those things won't define us. *Jesus will.*

"Whatever past achievements might bring us honor, whatever past disgraces might make us blush, all have been crucified with Christ and exist no more except in the deep recesses of eternity."[4]

᷎᷍

Jesus deeply understood His identity with His Father. He knew that He wasn't made for this world; He came to fulfill His mission. He was merely passing through and He would be returning home again soon. Even though He would die before many would truly know who He was, He didn't waver in His knowledge that He was *royalty*.

Because He knew His royalty and intimate oneness with God were not up for grabs or changeable with popular opinion, He was free to live and give Himself for others. He was always a King. But when He got up from the table to reach for that basin, He was doing something that the lowliest slave would have done. He put himself in the most humble position and proceeded to rub the dirt off the feet of those who looked to Him for leadership.

Jesus washed the disciples' feet, and yet He did far more than fulfill a predinner ritual. When Jesus put His hands into that blackened basin, He showed us the secret to seeing others as He sees them. We are taught from this significant act how to really love the unlovely . . . even if that unlovely person is the one staring back at us in the mirror.

People are not what they *do* . . . they are someone God loves. *We* are not what we do . . . we are someone He enjoys. In big things and small things, amidst productive seasons and desolate ones, whether surrounded by loving friends or hostile enemies, we are His treasure, and that *never* changes.

When we understand that we were created for His beautiful purpose, our eyes become more focused on what matters. We become enveloped in His relentless love for us, and we get passionate about where He is taking us. We expect to encounter a few bumps along the way, but we finally believe that bumps, bruises, and deep valleys are not defining factors for us. Yes, they mark our journey and shape us into beautiful women, but they do not have the power to diminish our value.

We are nothing without Him, and everything to Him. We are a speck of dust in a vast and endless universe, and yet it pleases Him to stoop down to make us great (see Psalm 18:35).

It takes courage to accept acceptance. It takes grit to get up off the ground when we've been knocked down. It takes great humility to answer the high call when we've been the one throwing stones. And yet, this is the way of the saint; pressing onward and upward, not because of our perfection, because of His.

Faith is a living, daring confidence in God's grace. It is so sure and certain that a man could stake his life on it a thousand times.[5]
MARTIN LUTHER

To be uncommon is to silence the voice of our accuser that we may listen to the Lord's whisper. To be uncommon is to embrace the Lord's discipline that we may become more like Him. The uncommon woman refuses to let her mistakes or weaknesses define her because she is defined by His strengths alone.

Precious Lord,
You are all that I need. Somehow, I will learn to walk in this truth. Take everything about me and make me new again! Release me from the snare of others' opinions that I may serve You alone. Fill me up with a

*greater sense of my identity in You! Give me the
courage to take the leap of faith to believe that I am
someone You love. You are a sincere and faithful God,
and You deserve my highest affections. Be my highest
aim and my deepest love. Be my anchor and my sail. Be
my everything today and always, precious Lord Jesus.
I love You so. Amen.*

Declaration:
I declare, in Jesus' Name, that I am fully loved and
completely accepted! I have all that I need because
Christ lives in me! I refuse to look down or to lose
ground because of others' opinions or my past fail-
ings. God has redeemed my past and secured my
future so I can be alive and fruitful today. I accept
my high calling—and I, by faith, accept the fact that
I am accepted . . . completely! Amen.

what about you?

1. Have you ever considered that insecurity is just another form of selfishness? When we doubt our identity, we make choices with "me" in mind. Most of
   what we do then becomes an effort to rescue our
   sense of self-worth. Read 1 Corinthians 7:23. Describe a time when you were tripped up by someone
   else's perception of you. What was the underlying
   lie that you believed?

2. Write down the initials (or a code word to protect your privacy) of those whose opinions matter to you to a fault. Ask forgiveness. Spend some time entrusting yourself once again to the Lord. Ask Him to give you a renewed perspective.

3. Most of us have "solid ground" areas where we walk with a measure of holy confidence, and yet we also have "sinking sand" areas that make it hard for us to remember who we are. What are the defining differences between your "solid ground" and your "sinking sand" areas? Write them down.

4. How can you carry the holy confidence (to which you were called) outside your familiar territory—to places unknown—without falling into the quicksand of insecurity? What are some precautions you might take? Write down a few of your ideas.

5. Read 1 John 4:16. The Greek word for "know" in this verse is *ginosko*, which, among other things, is a Jewish idiom for sexual intercourse between a man and a woman.⁶ Think about that for a moment. To "know this love" is to be so acquainted with Jesus' affections for you that more than anything else in all the earth you identify yourself as someone who is loved. Beyond titles, labels, mistakes, or accomplishments . . . you are absolutely treasured by the One who knows it all. Oh, that you may know this kind of love! What primarily defines you? Be honest.

6. The next word in this verse is "rely" or "believe." You believe your car will start when you put the key

in the ignition. You rely on your chair to hold you when you sit down. And yet, how much do you rely, count on, and believe in His love? What are some tangible ways you can more freely rely on His love (e.g., less bragging, more trusting, less worrying, more faith, less spending, more giving)? Write down your thoughts.

7. Write a prayer that reflects the things you want to say to the One who loves you.

God is your greatest fan.
As your heavenly Father,
He is constantly coaxing you forward
into the heights of spiritual victory. [1]

      ✑BOB SORGE

For the Lord your God is going with you!
He will fight for you against your enemies,
and he will give you victory!

      ✑DEUTERONOMY 20:4 NLT

chapter two

gets back up again

My first real fight caught me by surprise. I didn't see it coming. I was about nine years old and making my way home after school one day. Walking across a baseball field, I shuffled my feet through the dirt until I came to the grass. As I looked up I noticed my house was about fifty yards away.

From behind me I heard, "Get her!" Suddenly I went to the ground under the crashing weight of four teenage boys. My face landed in the dirt as they pushed off me to stand up. They kicked me and slugged me as they laughed wildly. One of them grabbed a fistful of my face as he gouged his fingernails into my cheek. I wailed and cried and fought to get up, but I was outnumbered and overpowered.

Out of the corner of my eye, I noticed a neighbor kid standing on the sidewalk with his arms at this side.

I screamed, "Help!"

He just stood there and didn't move.

I screamed again, "Help! Go get someone!"

He did nothing.

While I am sure the beating only lasted a couple of minutes, it felt like a couple of days. When the boys decided they were done, they took off running and disappeared somewhere in the neighborhood. I was lying in a heap with dirt in my teeth, a bloody lip, a scratched face, snarled hair, and an extremely achy body.

I waited until they were gone before I got up and made my way home. Then I plopped down on the couch, leaned into the arms of my mom, and began to cry.

⊙

That was over thirty years ago, and yet I still remember it as if it were yesterday. I remember how small and insignificant I felt. I remember how much I hated those boys even though I didn't know them. I didn't think there was anything to be learned from that dreadful moment in time. But I was wrong.

I felt justified in my hatred for the boys who beat me up. I also greatly feared them. But when I was a child, I thought like a child. Thanks to the love of Jesus, I would one day learn that *hatred and fear were things that would keep me down . . . not set me free*. Eventually I embraced the truth that I was called, anointed, and appointed for freedom. *So are you.* It doesn't matter how many times we've landed in the dirt—it just matters that we get back up again.

In fact, I've yet to meet or read about an uncommon woman who *hasn't* been knocked down by a bully or just by life.

Diane was repeatedly abused by her husband both physically and emotionally. She escaped with her children and her life. With a couple of true friends at her side and a God-sized conviction to change the world, Diane trusted God, took on her fears and, one step at a time, grew into someone who now ministers to women. She founded a shelter for battered women, and she currently organizes huge outreach programs for the poor.

Shelly is a pastor's wife and was verbally torn up and tossed aside by gossipy women in her congregation. She didn't leave the ministry—she ran to Jesus—and eventually poured her heart into a new group of women at a new church. Instead of growing cynical, she grew more passionate about a woman's need for freedom in Christ. Every time she opens her mouth, pearls of pure wisdom are offered to those who are listening.

Karen was in grade school when a group of kids her age repeatedly spit on her, shoved her around, and told her she was worthless. One day they locked her in a closet and then went out for recess. Her most painful memory was when she sat on the playground swing and watched as three janitors worked to scrub the words "Karen s—ks" off of the school building.

In her adult years, Karen fought hard to put that "worthless" lie under her feet. Through the power of the Holy Spirit and some godly mentors, Karen's whole life has been redeemed. She forgave her bullies and now serves as a youth pastor. She pours her life into training and teaching youth to be God-fearing and God-honoring people.

Brenda was a child when a man from her neighborhood assaulted her. As a godly young woman she spent much time in the Word but couldn't get a hold on the assurance that she was completely loved and thoroughly accepted by God.

At the prompting of some godly friends and due to a fresh perspective from the Word, Brenda decided to jump into the rivers of God's love and fully entrust her fears to Him. She turned her back on her fears and took the leap of faith to believe the truth about herself. Now she regularly teaches and mentors women. She also serves as a mighty intercessor for her church.

Carrie was regularly slapped, kicked, and punched . . . by her mother. She was locked in closets and sometimes in the bathroom for an entire day. She was molested by her grandfather and her brother. After she left home, she decided that she never wanted children because she was afraid she would mess them up somehow.

Because of the love of a devoted man and a faithful God, Carrie is now a beloved wife and the mother of four beautiful children. Carrie *stopped the cycle* and started a new heritage. Her children know they are loved, and together they've become a strong, solid family!

One way or another, these women got back up, brushed themselves off, and found the courage to find life-changing strength in the presence of God. They refused to be defined or limited by their pasts because they had their eyes on the promise of a hopeful future (see Jeremiah 29:11). Out of their battles emerged a conviction not only to walk in the truth of who they are—but to *be* a blessing and make a difference in the lives of others.

These women came through the fire without smelling like smoke. They were knocked down like many people are. But somehow they knew that in order to respond to the high and uncommon call on their lives, they *had* to get up, they *had* to forgive, and they *had* to believe that God's promises were still true for them. The fight to get up again is a good fight indeed.

～◎◎

As I have studied the life of Jesus, the depth of His character has continually overwhelmed me. *Everything* He did, *everything* He went through, was *for* something. When I think back to that time on the baseball field, I remember someone who stood at a safe distance while I took a beating. When it came right down to it, he wasn't going to risk getting hurt for me even though I was outnumbered and outsized. Because he didn't help me, I believed that I would always be at the mercy of my circumstances and that no one would ever stop bullies from being bullies.

But then I picture the scene before Jesus' crucifixion; I see the

Savior lying in the dirt with fistfuls of His beard ripped out and spit on His face; I imagine Him surrounded by mockers and tormentors . . . and I realize He did the much harder thing. In fact, He did for me what I could not do for myself.

He defeated my foe. He won the war. And He secured my victory. He made a way for every person who has ever been knocked down to get back up again.

At the point of our belief, we were given access to all of the provision, protection, and promise we would ever need to win our battles. Satan would love to lead us into conflicts that we cannot win, but with Jesus at our side, we cannot lose. By His great wisdom He hides us when we shouldn't fight, strengthens us when we should, and trains us for our next level of service.

Though hard times come and people are cruel, we don't have to live tormented by our fears, nor do we have to be forever impaired by our past defeats. The more we understand who and whose we are, the more we'll truly believe that God will restore *every* lost thing. We'll comprehend which battles are ours for the taking and when it's good just to hide in the shadow of His wing and rest awhile. Jesus loves us so much and always has a watchful eye on us. Here's what He says:

"My sheep listen to my voice; I know them, and they follow me. I give them eternal life, and they will never perish. No one can snatch them away from me, for my Father has given them to me, and he is more powerful than anyone else. No one can snatch them from the Father's hand" (John 10:27–29 NLT).

❧

The Bible says that in the last days, the love of many will grow cold. If we are to live as Christ did—and not become one of the many—we will need to forgive the unforgivable (more on this later). When the messes of life wound us and knock us down, we will need the courage to get back up again. Even though our pain will at times seem more real than God's presence, we must trust Him.

It's okay if we start out with an unassertive handle on what we possess in Christ, as long as we keep on moving, keep on trusting, keep on believing. Eventually, we will come to grips with our divine potential because we will believe in our very core that God is divinely interested and involved with us.

The fibers in our very beings will know it; the nerves running through our bodies will know it; even the people in our sphere of influence will know that we know that we are somebody to God.

It's true that from the galaxy's perspective, we are like little dust mites living on a relatively small planet. But truer still is that God knows us by name. Even though He oversees the affairs of the whole universe, He knows if we're having a good hair day or a bad one. Every hair is numbered. Every fluttering sparrow outside is on His radar. We are His treasure, and the sooner we believe it, the sooner we will rise to the uncommon call to live with holy confidence and humble dependence.

Humility will not be far from us, because we will always remember Jesus, the basin, and His disciples; and we will serve from a humbly confident heart. Getting back up again will always be an option because we know Jesus to be a mighty warrior who will defend us at every turn.

When we would prefer to judge people who irritate us, we will remember our own murky water sloshing around in the basin. When we find ourselves striving for position and self-importance, we will remember how God's only Son rubbed between our toes and then asked us to do the same for others. When we doubt our importance and value, we will remember how the Savior of the world became a servant so that we could become clean.

Jesus led by example; He showed us how to walk, how to live, and how to love. When He was accused, He didn't become insecure; He already knew who He was. When He was mistreated, He didn't fight back; He saw past it. When He should have turned His back on us all, He instead prayed, "Father, forgive them, for they don't know what they are doing."

In a day and age when our unalienable rights have become somehow sacred, we must remember what Jesus did. He loved, He forgave, and He put evil under His feet.

What kind of change could be affected in our world if we, as Christ's followers, had lines we wouldn't cross no matter what *anyone* else was doing or saying? If we could remain kind while others are cruel, if we could keep from hating while others do dreadful things—are there any bounds to what the Lord could do through us?

No matter how the enemy has tried to knock you down, whether by sickness or betraying friends, by past fears or current financial hardships, God can lift you up again and make something beautiful of your life.

Your fingers might be cramped from dragging your past with you, but loosen your grip and give your baggage, once and for all, to the One who knows you and cherishes you.

> *God brings no woman into the conflicts of life to desert her. Every woman has a Friend in Heaven whose resources are unlimited; and on Him she may call at any hour and find sympathy and assistance.*[2]

Get a vision for what is possible for the uncommon woman in you. Ask yourself, "What would every other woman do with my set of circumstances?" and then raise your standard. Dare to ask the Lord, "What would *You* do with this mess I call my life? With You at my side, what kind of mark could *I* make in this world?"

And to that your Beloved would answer, "*Anything* is possible."

Read this wonderful verse from Proverbs 15:24 (NLT):

"The path of life leads upward for the wise; they leave the grave behind."

Dear Father in Heaven,
I need You every hour. Strengthen me according to Your
Word. Fill me up with a glorious anticipation for what
You want to do in my life! Make me spiritually savvy
enough to walk around the traps set for me by the
enemy. May I turn my back on fear and embrace faith
instead. When I get knocked down, help me to get back
up again. May the destiny You've appointed for me be
forever in my view. I want to be a woman who rises up
out of the ashes and does something beautiful with her
life. Do Your work in me, Lord. Amen.

Declaration:
I declare, in Jesus' Name, that no weapon formed against me will prosper and that every tongue that rises up against me will be proven to be false (see Isaiah 54:17). I refuse to be bound by past defeats or daily insecurities. I belong to Jesus, and He is making all things new in my life! I will not allow the enemy of my soul to bully me with fears and discouragement. I will hold on to courage and a strong faith in the Almighty. I will live a life worthy of my calling because Jesus has already won my victory!

what about you?

1. Read 2 Samuel 22:2–4. Read it again slowly, and think about how this passage applies to you. List every descriptive word written about God (e.g., rock, refuge, and others). In your own words, describe each of these words as it relates to God's attention toward us.

2. Which of these do you most identify with right now? Do you need Him to be your protector? Do you need Him to hide you away for a while? Describe.

3. Read verses 5 and 6. Describe a time in your life when these words applied to you.

4. Read verse 7. Read it again. Isn't it amazing? From His temple, He heard you. Write a short prayer telling God what that means to you.

5. Read verses 8–20. Note that God was angry because you were in distress. He was angry with your enemies. Notice the power with which He executes His plans. There is no one like our God! Tell Him so.

6. Read verses 29–37 and rewrite this passage in prayer form (e.g., "I thank You, Lord, that with Your help, I can . . . ").

*Have courage for the great
sorrows of life and patience for
the small ones; and when you have
laboriously accomplished your daily task,
go to sleep in peace.
God is awake.*

❧ VICTOR HUGO

Who is this King-Glory?
God, armed and battle-ready.

❧ PSALM 24:8 THE MESSAGE

wisely picks
her battles

Have you ever ended up at a dinner party with someone you know doesn't like you? How did you handle it? Did you laugh extra loud so that she would know you were having a great time? Or did you slip into the background and blend in with the antiques and the nondescript wallpaper? Or maybe you are the bold type, and you walked right up to her and settled things once and for all, even if it wasn't the most opportune place.

Jesus has been there. He was at His own dinner party with eleven friends and one enemy (see John 13:2). He had legions of angels at His beck and call, and yet He was not calling for them. Since He was a master communicator, He could have talked circles around Judas and made him look the fool. Or He could have confronted Judas head-on and exposed him for the traitor he was. But He didn't even do that.

Jesus was so in tune with the Father that He wouldn't make a move without Him. And the message His Father was giving Him at that moment was this: "Entrust yourself to Me and love them. Tenderly wash the grime off of their feet so they will remember how You came and how You lived. Judas will soon receive the judgment due him, and You will receive the glory due Your Holy Name."

Jesus was God and yet He did nothing without the Father's instruction.

> Jesus gave them this answer: "I tell you the truth, the Son can do nothing by himself; he can do only what he sees his Father doing, because whatever the Father does the Son also does." (John 5:19)

> As if Jesus' example wasn't enough for us, He passed along this same lesson when He said to us, "Apart from me you can do nothing." (see John 15:5)

◌◌

One day while reading the book of Ruth, I was struck by Boaz's instruction to Ruth. "Listen, my daughter. Stay right here with us when you gather grain; don't go to any other fields. Stay right behind the young women working in my field. See which part of the field they are harvesting, and then follow them. I have warned the young men not to treat you roughly. And when you are thirsty, help yourself to the water they have drawn from the well" (Ruth 2:8–9 NLT).

During my prayer time I cradled my cup of coffee, looked out the window, and pondered Boaz's protection of Ruth. I sensed the whisper across my own heart: *My daughter, stay within the boundaries I have set for you. You are safe here. My strong right arm will protect you as we take on certain battles together. If you venture out beyond where I have told you to go, you will be subjecting yourself to the wiles of the enemy. Stay close to Me; I will help you avoid the enemy's snares; I will help you to remember who you are; stand strong when I tell you to; drink from My well, and you'll have all that you need.*

You see, not every battle is ours to fight. Not every wrong is ours to right. Jesus has so specifically ordained our lives that we will *each* encounter different seasons at different times. For you, this may be a time to recover. For another, this may be a time to take cover. And still another might be called to run *to* the battle line.

Some will have peace in their homes while there is war on the streets. Others may feel like their home *is* the war zone while those around them live seemingly peaceful lives. If we stay in step with our Savior, we will know when it is time to raise our shield and draw our sword and when it is time to step back and wait, drawing from His well and being filled back up again. Always, though, it's *God's* shield we raise; it's His victory we proclaim, and it's His right hand that lifts us up to a new and better place.

> You give me your shield of victory, and your right hand sustains me; you stoop down to make me great. (Psalm 18:35)

We as women get anxious and weary when we hoist the world's problems onto our own shoulders. God is already carrying the world, so we don't have to. We only have to carry what *He* puts in our hands for that day. And while Jesus promised that in this world we would have trouble, He encouraged us to smile anyway, because *He* has overcome the world (see John 16:33).

In every battle God remains the Most High God—over all of our circumstances—with us in every season. He defends us. He fights for us. And He delivers us. Did you know that it's possible to live peacefully and be victorious in battle at the same time?

> Praise be to the Lord my Rock, who trains my hands for war, my fingers for battle. He is my loving God and my fortress, my stronghold and my deliverer, my shield, in whom I take refuge, who subdues peoples under me. (Psalm 144:1–2)

Victory and refuge are both yours. Peace is offered to you at all times in all ways. You may be encountering conflict all around you. You may be tempted to fix things on your own. Don't make a move without Jesus. Remember, too, that it's in these very times of vulnerability and misunderstanding that Jesus loves to make His presence known. Unfortunately, He removes His hands from the conflict if we insist on going into battle without Him.

Read this great excerpt from a book by author and pastor, Rick Renner:

> As you face your own challenges in life, always keep in mind that Jesus has the power to fix any problem you'll ever come across. Before you jump in and make things worse by taking matters into your own hands, remember the story of Peter (see Luke 22:49–51)! The next time you're tempted to "grab a sword and start swinging," take a few minutes to remind yourself that Jesus can handle the problem without your intervention. Before you do anything else, pray and ask the Lord what you are supposed to do. Then after you receive your answer and follow His instructions, just watch His supernatural power swing into action to solve the dilemma you are facing! [1]

We stay in the boundaries God has set for us when we settle in our minds that He is our great Defender. He won't lead us into battles we cannot win, and when we position ourselves within His stronghold, and we listen to His voice, we'll find in Him a place where we can *rest* secure; a place where we can *recline* at the table in the presence of our enemies.

"If you make the Most High your dwelling—even the Lord, who is my refuge—then no harm will befall you, no disaster will come near your tent. . . . You will tread upon the lion and the cobra; you will trample the great lion and the serpent. 'Because (she) loves me,' says the Lord, 'I will rescue (her); I will protect (her), for (she) acknowledges my name. (She) will call upon me, and I will answer (her); I will be with (her) in trouble, I will deliver (her) and honor (her)'" (Psalm 91:9–10; 13–15).

⁃ꙮ⁃

How do we choose our battles wisely? We humbly stay in step with Jesus and consider Him our greatest Defender. We hold ourselves to the high standard that He modeled for us. We determine ahead of time which conflicts are beneath us (e.g., building a case against someone, disputing over trivial differences, and so on). We put safeguards around our hearts and minds, and we keep our lives free from the clutter of gossip, drama, and pettiness.

In the next chapter we will explore five battles the uncommon woman must be willing to *engage* in so she can *gain ground* in her walk of faith. But let's first establish which battles we're *not* called to so that we might not *lose ground*. A high percentage of the conflicts in which we find ourselves are not God-ordained battles; they are potholes in our path, prepared for us by the enemy. They are the little "self traps" that will trip us up, steal our time, drain our joy, and take us from the higher road if we allow them to. The sooner we can get over ourselves and thus learn to walk around such traps, the sooner we will get on to the better things in life.

We are not called to: Defend every ill word spoken of us

For some reason, most women love to snack on the dainty morsels of gossip. It appears such a small thing to toss a few words around; at least it seems so until you find that those who are talking *to* you are also talking *about* you. That's when you realize those seemingly harmless morsels are actually laced with arsenic.

Women are going to talk. Some of those words will get back to us. The enemy intends for those words to hit their mark and injure us. He would love to generate a wrong response from us. If he can't get us to crumble in a heap, he will try to get us to come out swinging. If we're not the fighting type, he'll prod us to take every opportunity to defend ourselves and make our accusers look as bad as they are—or at least as bad as they seem.

We've no doubt each responded in one or more of these ways before, and yet these responses are beneath God's highest and best for us. Let's look at Jesus' response to cruelty:

"He was oppressed and treated harshly, yet he never said a word. He was led like a lamb to the slaughter. And as a sheep is silent before the shearers, he did not open his mouth" (Isaiah 53:7 NLT).

When we are caught in the dust storm of accusation, betrayal, and rejection, the best thing we can do is hold our ground and wait for the Lord. No one knows the pain of ill-spoken words like Jesus, and when we entrust ourselves to Him, He becomes our greatest Defender. Besides, it just looks bad to see a woman attempt to rescue her sense of worth as if she has somehow lost it (trust me; I've seen myself do it before and it wasn't pretty).

On the other hand, it's a powerful sight indeed when a godly woman holds her words and her ground in the face of cruelty. That woman will surely be vindicated in due time.

A. W. Tozer penned a compelling passage on this topic (I reworded this quotation for women):

The meek woman is not a human mouse afflicted with a sense of her own inferiority. Rather, she may be in her moral life as bold as a lion and as strong as Samson; but she has stopped being fooled about herself. She has accepted God's estimate of her own life. She knows she is as weak and helpless as God has declared her to be, but paradoxically, she knows at the same time that she is, in the sight of God, more important than the angels. In herself, nothing; in God, everything. That is her motto. She knows well that the world will never see her as God sees her and she has stopped caring.

She rests perfectly content to allow God to place His own values. She will be patient to wait for the day when everything will get its own price tag and real worth will come into its own. Then the righteous shall shine forth in the kingdom of their Father. She is willing to wait for that day. In the meantime, she will have attained a place of soul rest. As she walks on in meekness she will be happy to let God defend her. The old struggle to defend herself is over. She has found the peace that meekness brings.[2]

How wonderful it is to be free from the desire to control what other people say about us! Trying to prevent others from having low conversations and engaging in petty gossip about us is like trying to keep the leaves from falling off of the trees on a windy fall day. Why attempt an impossible feat that will turn us upside down with worry and make us lose perspective? We have better things to do!

Just how *do* we stay away from this battlefield?

We regularly pray:

Father, Thank You, by faith, for hiding me in the shelter of Your presence, safe from those who conspire against me. Thank You for sheltering me in Your presence, far from accusing tongues. (See Psalm 31:20.)

In other words, we daily and prayerfully declare, "I don't need to hear what others are saying about me; I need to be regularly reminded of what *Jesus* says about me. I am His and He is mine. His banner over me is love."

We also regularly pray:

Surround me with people who tremble at Your word and fear Your holy name. May all who fear You find in me a cause for joy, for I have put my hope in You. (See Psalm 119:74.)

In other words, we daily and prayerfully declare, "I won't attempt to reason with those who have no inner conviction to be holy and honorable in the way they conduct themselves. But for those who *do* walk in the fear of the Lord, may *they* find in me a cause for joy—may they witness in me the Living God—for I have put my hope in Him."

We pray. We stay close to Him. And we choose our friends wisely.

Sometimes no matter what standards you make or precautions you take, hurtful words will still find their way to you. I spent a number of years declaring Scripture, watching my tongue, and praying for my enemies before I was totally free from the effects of my own character assassination. In due time I was surrounded by faithful, God-fearing friends, and there was no room in any of our lives for that sort of thing.

But lo and behold, one day a woman who was a friend of a friend, wanted to meet me. She, my friend, and I were going to ride together to a Bible study; we all thought that this would be a great chance to connect. Something came up the night of the Bible study and my friend couldn't make it. Within minutes of hopping into the car with a woman I didn't know, she was telling me that she knew my former friends and proceeded to tell me how terribly they talked about me.

Before I had the chance to hear the gory details, I put my hand up and said, "Stop right now. I don't want to hear it. I've invested countless hours in prayer so that I would be able to forgive and bless these people. Now that this can of worms is opened again, we are going to pray for them." Right then and there, I bowed my head and prayed for my beloved enemies.[3] I won that one.

My friend's friend was not the enemy. My former friends were not the enemy. My battle wasn't against flesh and blood, but against the spiritual forces of evil in the heavenly realm (see

Ephesians 6:12). The devil wanted to lure me out of my freedom and back into the captivity of others' opinions. Thankfully the precious Holy Spirit helped me to stay on the high road.

Though the "skirmish" came to me, I entrusted myself to the Lord. God met me there and I was reminded once again of how much I detest the "she said, she said" conversations. Moreover, my heart was filled anew with the thought of how noble and beautiful and lovely the way is for the one who trusts in Him.

We are not called to: Walk in the fear of man

I remember one day many years ago when during a time of prayer, the Lord whispered across my heart, *Susie, I want there to be a bigger gap between how people affect you and how I affect you. My opinion should far outweigh the opinions of others.* I realized right then and there how bound I was by others' opinions of me. Proverbs says, "The fear of man brings a snare, but the fear of God brings safety" (see 29:25).

From that moment on, I began a higher pursuit of God. I learned the secret of renewing my mind. I prayed Scripture daily. I even "took sides against myself" at times by not allowing myself to lift a finger for the wrong reasons. If my motive was to rescue my sense of self-worth, I instead took my empty self to the Lord and asked Him to fill me back up again.

Something amazing started to happen. Peace and security filled in the gaps of my life where turmoil and insecurity used to be. By refusing to entertain even a single thought about what others might be thinking of me, and instead filling my mind with the wonder of God's love, everything in me and around me changed. Each day I took a step in the right direction. Eventually I tiptoed onto the edges of my promised land. I felt freedom's grass between my toes; I breathed in the pure air of unpolluted acceptance; I ran through my very own fields of grace, and I determined that I would never again return to my captivity.

How *do* we know if we are held captive by others' opinions?

❖ *When our thoughts are consumed with others' thoughts toward us*—we are walking in the fear of man.

❖ *When our day goes south because we feel slighted by a comment or a cross look*—we are walking in the fear of man.

❖ *When we feel the need to get others on our side by speaking ill of another* —we are walking in the fear of man.

❖ *When our goal is more to impress than to bless*—we are walking in the fear of man.

Fear of others' opinions doesn't just show itself through insecurity—it's also revealed through pride (which is another form of insecurity, I suppose). There's no winning the battle of others' opinions. It's a trap, and we will be its slave if we reduce our lives to a series of actions that will please others and give them a *momentary* favorable opinion of us.

However, when we walk in the fear of the Lord—when we love Him enough to do what He says—we will be safe. Not that others won't gossip—they will—but when they do, He will be our defense.

To walk in the fear of the Lord is to say, "Help *me* not to gossip, Lord. Help *me* to make choices from a place of fullness, not emptiness. Help *me* to believe that all I could ever need or want is found in You."

The Bible says that it's for freedom that Christ has set us free:

Christ has truly set us free. So take your stand! Never again let anyone put a harness of slavery on you. (Galatians 5:1 THE MESSAGE)

Christ died for it. He paid for it. And it's both our privilege *and* our responsibility to walk and live and breathe—free from the bondage of others' opinions. So, how exactly does freedom look on the uncommon woman?

❖ *When we sin and we are quick to repent to both God and man—* we are walking in the fear of the Lord.

❖ *When we are considerate of others' feelings without giving them the power to decide our value—*we are walking in the fear of the Lord.

❖ *When we are willing to step out in faith to places that are beyond our reach—regardless of the cynicism of others—*we are walking in the fear of the Lord.

❖ *When we pursue a holy, obedient life and entrust our reputation to the Lord Almighty—*we are walking in the fear of the Lord.

Where the Spirit of the Lord is, there is freedom!

Jesus came to earth for us because He loves us. But even *He* wouldn't hand over His identity to others:

I do not accept praise from men. (John 5:41)

Not that I accept human testimony; but I mention it that you may be saved. (John 5:34)

But Jesus would not entrust himself to them, for he knew all men. He did not need man's testimony about man, for he knew what was in a man. (John 2:24–25)

It is better to take refuge in the Lord than to trust in people. (Psalm 118:8 NLT)

We will be blessed with wonderful relationships along the way. We will be hurt by divisive people along the way. No matter.

We love people and we hope in God.

All around us are potential conflicts waiting to happen. We find freedom when we no longer need to defend ourselves. We avoid needless battles when we step off the low road of gossip and insecurity. Our footsteps become lighter when we shake free from the need to make sure everyone understands us. God understands us and that's enough.

> *Freedom in Christ produces a healthy independence from peer pressure, people-pleasing, and the bondage of human respect. The tyranny of public opinion can manipulate our lives. What will the neighbors think? What will my friends think? . . . In Christ Jesus freedom from fear empowers us to let go of the desire to appear good, so that we can move freely in the mystery of who we really are.*[4]
>
> BRENNAN MANNING

Dear Father,

How wonderful are Your truths! I long to see myself the way You do! Fill me up afresh with an understanding of who I am to You. You carry the world on Your shoulders so I don't have to. Help me to walk away from conflicts that are Yours to handle. If I fight for anything. may it be for faith, hope, and love. When others come against me, You will be my defense. When evil words find their way to me, You will teach me how to pray. And when I am tempted to prove to the world that I am something, You will hide me in the shadow of Your wing. Give me wisdom when confronted with conflict. Bring a new freedom to me, Lord. Help me to love others, but to put my hope in You. Amen.

Declaration:

I declare, in the Name of Jesus, that I am complete in Christ! I have discernment in how I relate to others, and I wisely walk away from the battles God has not called me to fight. I will not be bound or manipulated by others' opinions of me. Even when good people think I am bad, I will put my trust in Him. I refuse to look down, look back, or wonder about my worth, because it is a settled issue! I will not engage in spiteful conversations, nor will I listen to gossip about anybody. I refuse thoughts of insecurity, and I will not engage in petty differences that will ruin my day! I am made for better things. I will love, I will forgive, and I will walk in the fullness Christ has made available to me.

what about you?

1. First Samuel 15 tells us about a time when King Saul received instruction from the Lord through Samuel. Saul was given clear instructions to go into battle and wipe out the enemy. Saul only partially obeyed. Read 1 Samuel 15:16–17 (NLT) and notice Samuel's words to Saul. "Although you may think little of yourself, are you not the leader of the tribes of Israel?" It's as if Samuel is saying, "Do you see the danger of minimizing who God has made you to be? Don't you see the impact of your choices when you think wrongly about whom you are and what you're called to?" Apply this to your own life. Make the

connection between your full obedience and the importance of understanding just who you are. Write down your thoughts.

2. In what ways do you minimize your own value and then make light of small departures and subtle sins that you know are beneath you? Write them down.

3. Read verse 24 where Saul gives the reason for his disobedience. Think about the consequences of his actions for a moment. Ponder the cost of fearing man versus fearing God. Write down your thoughts.

4. Read Isaiah 8:13. Describe a battle or a conflict you were tripped up by because you feared the wrong thing.

5. Read Proverbs 12:16. How do you currently handle insults? Is there an even higher road that you can take?

6. "The righteous choose their friends carefully, but the way of the wicked leads them astray" (Proverbs 12:26 TNIV). Are there any ways God is calling you to be more cautious in your friendships?

God has provided all we need to
defeat this adversary of ours—both
the enemy within and the enemy without.
We can triumph if we choose to employ
God's provision and obey His instructions.[1]
❧ QUIN SHERRER AND RUTHANNE GARLOCK

Live a life worthy of the calling
you have received.
❧ EPHESIANS 4:1

chapter four

forgives, receives, stands, bows, and perseveres

Have you ever washed someone's feet? Have you ever done so at great cost to yourself? I'm not talking about plopping your muddy toddler up onto the counter and putting his feet in the sink. I'm talking about getting on your knees in front of someone who has deeply wounded you . . . taking her feet into your hands . . . and tenderly washing them because God has given you the grace to do so.

Most of us haven't experienced such a moment, but let's imagine it anyway. Picture yourself gently holding and washing your offender's feet while praying a prayer of blessing for her; hear yourself sincerely asking for God's mercy on her behalf. Imagine walking with your offender into the Lord's most holy chamber with your arm around her—interceding for her in the same way Christ intercedes for you. Feel the freedom and the divine influence that surrounds you as you stand in the gap in an otherworldly, beyond-your-time sort of way.

If you have Jesus in you, you have it in you to walk this way:

loving, forgiving, and interceding for those who don't get you, who have hurt you, and who don't deserve your love. You have it in you to be tough against the lies of the enemy and tender toward the things of God. You believe God is faithful and you throw all of your hope, your dreams, and your faith into the fact that He *will* come through for you in time. You are humble enough to receive God's grace, and gracious enough to give it.

And as you walk this way, *do know* that you are on the path and following the footsteps of some mighty men and women of God who have gone before you. The path of standing strong despite conflict, standing in the gap for those who don't deserve it; the path of forgiveness, of intercession, and of relying on the faithfulness of God has been paved by such greats as Moses, Joseph, Esther, David, and Jesus, just to name a few. Yours is an uncommon call indeed.

Our Deliverer has come. He came, He served, He died, and He *rose again* that we might live free and powerful lives. Death passed over us, but not just death—the bondage of sin, the drain of defeat, and the snare of others' opinions; cancerous unforgiveness, recurring insecurity, small dreams, constant fear, bland mediocrity, and sickening pettiness . . . all of these *can* be left behind us because the Name of Jesus is written on our hearts.

~ ❧ ~

The thing that continually amazes me about this Man Jesus is that He takes us—rags and all—and makes something of us. In His presence and by His leading, we turn from wimps to warriors, from being petty to powerful. He turns our lives upside down, and then He equips us to turn the world upside down.

We can stay the same if we want to, but one day we'll have to give an account for this decision. We can hold fast to our "right" to be comfortable and the demand that everybody treat us a certain way, but eventually we'll have to give an account.

But for those of us who are done with such things, we can rise to the occasion, engage in our appointed battles, and thereby move from being a "soft civilian" to a lean, highly trained, uncommon woman of God.

Here are the five battlegrounds to which every uncommon woman must tend (and on a regular basis), that she might continue to gain ground and consistently win her battles.

1. The battle to FORGIVE: "Therefore I tell you, whatever you ask for in prayer, believe that you have received it, and it will be yours. And when you stand praying, if you hold anything against anyone, forgive him, so that your Father in heaven may forgive you your sins" (Mark 11:24–25). Ooh, I love these verses. Look closer. Do you see the call to be uncommon here? Can you grasp what's been made available to those willing to take the higher road of holiness and forgiveness? (Hint: what you ask for in belief will be yours.)

Offered to us are the resources of heaven backed by the honor of God's Word. And why do we need *super*-natural assistance? Let me answer that one: because circumstances all around us beg for supernatural intervention. People today are all done with platitudes and clichés. They are not interested in clever-sounding stories; they want to be healed and restored. They want to be an eyewitness to God's majesty; they want to experience His power, and they want to know victory. They want to know that the Jesus you talk about is alive and active and willing to change their lives.

Augustine wrote, "Without God, we cannot. Without us, God will not." God has determined to work through us imperfect, but perfectly loved people. As far as it concerns us, we must be clean vessels for this beautiful work.

The importance of forgiveness cannot be overlooked here. Not only does un-forgiveness poison our souls and make our faces wrinkle like a crumpled up piece of paper, unforgiveness cuts us off from the very life source of promises needed to extend Christ's work on earth. When we stand on the side of unforgiveness, we stand against God. To stand against God is to turn our backs on Him and to cross over to the other side where we face Him as a foe rather than a Friend.

Jesus is a Friend to sinners. He positions Himself against the proud and the self-appointed judge. He draws near to the humble one, and when she cries out for mercy, she gets it from Him.

To fight for our "right" *not* to forgive is a struggle that will only weaken us. People will wound and betray us, it is true. But postponing our joy until *they* pay is like refusing to file an insurance claim because we want the actual burglar to bring back our money.

In the matters of our heart and our calling, our offender is beside the point. The fight for us is one for a heart that is willing to hand over our offenses because Jesus asks us to. God will defend. God will settle the accounts, and when He does, everyone will know that He is a God of righteousness and power. We don't need to instruct Him in the ways of justice.

Christian women for the most part, are willing to forgive the big offenses. But it's the little trifling things that we tend to carry with us. Sometimes it's embarrassing how petty we can be.

Last Sunday, my husband and I were serving Communion in church. We were singing Chris Tomlin's version of "Amazing Grace" where we proclaim, "My chains are gone; I've been set free. . . . " Suddenly I noticed our friend Moses in the front row, and I had an instant lump in my throat and tears in my eyes. Moses is a sweet man from Liberia.

Moses has known unspeakable pain and betrayal. What I'm about to write might make you wince, but I think it will provide an important perspective for us as women. Years ago, back in Liberia, Moses's brother was murdered. His body was hacked into pieces and thrown into a river.

Moses worked through his anger and the anguish caused by this horrific crime. One day he made the dangerous trip to the next town to confront his brother's killer. When the murderer saw Moses approaching, he assumed, "Surely this man has come to kill me for what I have done."

But Moses had made the trip so that he could tell this murderer face-to-face that he forgave him.

Moses has experienced things I cannot include in this book, but trust me: the physical and emotional scars are there. And so when I see him in the front row with his arms raised high and tears in his eyes as he sings, "My chains are gone; I've been set free . . . ", I know with all my heart that we as women have a much higher capacity for forgiveness than we even know.

The fight for what writer Francis Frangipane calls an "unoffendable heart"[2] is the fight in which the uncommon woman must engage. Countless stones will be tossed your way. Some will be intended to inflict pain. Others will be kicked at you unintentionally. Either way, you'll have a stone at your feet.

What will you do next?

Will you pick up that stone and throw it back? Will you pick it up, get a little mad, and then carry the offense with you? Or will you look at that stone and realize its potential to weigh you down and thus decide to let it go? Furthermore, do you have it in you to take the uncommon road and return a blessing instead?

This is no small or trivial battleground. This field is soaked with the precious blood of our Savior. He won the war of unforgiveness by forgiving us. We march on to victory and carry on His Kingdom work by being vessels of that *same forgiveness*. Receiving it and giving it. Receiving it and giving it. Receiving it again and giving it again.

If you are willing to regularly and continually fight the fight of forgiveness, you will have available to you untold blessing and answered prayer. Give God your best by giving Him the worst of all that's ever happened to you.

2. The battle to RECEIVE: "Receive and experience the amazing grace of the Master, Jesus Christ, deep, deep within yourselves" (Philippians 4:23 THE MESSAGE). It may be more blessed to give than receive, but it's also *easier* to give than it is to receive; at least it is for most of us.

Every once in a while, I go through a bout of insomnia, and when my sleep eludes me, so does my perspective. The enemy uses such times to remind me of every birdbrained, doofus thing I've ever said or done. As I toss and turn at night, my mind floods with memories of those I've hurt, bothered, or disappointed. I remember those who forgave me and blessed me, and yet as I lie all tangled up in my sheet, I tie myself up in knots again for past mistakes that I can't seem to get past. I then remember those who didn't want to forgive because they didn't want to give up their conversations in which they rehashed the issue.

I stare at the clock, which seems to have come to a grinding halt, and I feel sad and mad all at the same time. And since there are still more hours left in the night, I move on to worrying about who else I *might* offend tomorrow, or the next day, or the day after that.

This of course quickly morphs into the fear that I will quite likely offend God and He will most assuredly join the ranks of those who have been on the receiving end of my humanity and who didn't appreciate it very much. As you can tell, I am especially hard on myself when I'm tired. And when I'm this blind with exhaustion, I have a hard time finding my way to grace.

Maybe sleepless nights are not your issue. But we all have our susceptible moments when the enemy finds in us a vulnerable opening and then steps in to use it to his advantage. Maybe for you it's after you've been with the in-laws. Or maybe just after you've eaten too much, or talked too much, or charged too many items on your credit card. We all have times when the darkness of our souls is paraded in front of us and we're reminded once again how easily we can be moved from strength to weakness, from victory to defeat, from light to darkness.

But then the morning comes.

No matter how tired I am, I still love the morning. Every morning, I sit on my deck so I won't miss a thing. I love the pillars of light that shine through the trees making me feel like I'm in an outdoor cathedral. I love the ever-changing canvas we call the sky. I look up and I'm reminded once again that God truly is amazing. And even though I'm not fond of long, cold winters, I love winter mornings when the sun shines and the flakes fall, and songbirds sing . . . all at the same time.

What does this have to do with receiving, you ask? Everything! His mercies are *new* every morning and His faithfulness is great. He gives, He gives, and He gives again. Yes, we've made mistakes in the past and we will make mistakes again. And just a side note: the enemy has no right to bring up past sin that's been forgiven by Jesus. He'll camp on the assumption that we don't know our rights until we hold up our legal document (the Bible) and tell him to be gone in Jesus' name!

But still, how do we wrap our arms around grace when we are blatantly aware of our sinful nature? This is especially important for the uncommon woman because, as Joyce Meyer says, "New level, new devil." In other words, as we climb, we will face different kinds of opposition, and the enemy will do everything he can to get us to look down. Somehow we have to find ways to quickly put these attacks under our feet; otherwise, our joy will constantly be at the mercy of our choices and our perspective.

I think I found an answer for us. In the Song of Songs, the Shulammite is the beautiful woman who is being wooed by her king into a love relationship. She so desperately wants intimacy with her king, but she is also reminded of the reasons why she is not suited for this wonderful love relationship. Yet still, she finds it in her to say, "Dark am I, yet lovely" (1:5).

Read what author and Pastor Brian Simmons wrote about this passage:

> Throughout life, every new "chamber room" experience will bring an even deeper understanding of unworthiness. You will cry out each time, "O, Lord: I am darkened by my sin." But if you listen carefully, you will also hear the King say, "Yet lovely!" The voice she hears from the shadows whispers to her: "You may seem dark, but you are lovely to Me!" Imagine the King bringing you into His chambers . . . Not to tell you what is wrong with you, but to tell you how lovely you are![3]

It takes a certain toughness in the face of weakness to turn a deaf ear to the enemy and open your heart once again to Christ's relentless grace. This is what I do, and it works every time. When I encounter an onslaught of condemnation brought on by a bout of insomnia, I look up and *make myself smile*. (Do it right now. Make yourself smile. Doesn't it feel great?) Then I simply say, "I'm so tired, Lord. Oh, but You love me. There's no condemnation in my life because I am Yours, You are mine, and Your banner over me is love. I will take this opportunity to rest in You."

And just like clockwork, I hear His sweet voice whisper back, *Wide is the road of grace beneath your feet. I've got you.*

To move into the bigger and the deeper and the more profound things of God, we must continuously and relentlessly hang on to grace and divine love. Daily He's pouring it out; daily we must *receive* a fresh dose of it. Every morning, He's there. Open your hands.

3. The battle to STAND: "Stay alert! Watch out for your great enemy, the devil. He prowls around like a roaring lion,

looking for someone to devour. Stand firm against him, and be strong in your faith" (1 Peter 5:8–9 NLT). Proverbs 4:23 tells us to guard our hearts with all *diligence* (NKJV) because of this truth: whatever we allow in our hearts, we allow in our lives, which determines the path we take and the choices we make. The word "diligence" in this verse is from the Hebrew word *mishmar*,[4] which is akin to the stance that a guard would have protecting a prison, or a man would have defending his land from intruders.

Think for a minute about the prison guard or a man protecting his homestead. Imagine him *standing* at attention, holding his weapon, tuning his ears to the slightest sounds, and keeping his eyes open to what is going on all around him.

We tend to think of these roles as "men's" jobs, although that's no longer the case. We live in a different era. Even so, it's far too easy to dismiss this almost masculine call for diligence as something that doesn't apply to us.

Please don't misunderstand me to say that we must lose our femininity. On the contrary. Nothing is more beautiful than a woman who is fully feminine and yet strong in the things of God. She quickly bows her knee before her Maker, and just as quickly *stands* against the lies that would devour her family. She works hard at forgiveness and perseveres with great strength through the storm. The uncommon woman is someone of unique femininity *and* great strength.

The fight to stand is the fight to say *no* to insecurity, fear, defeat, and discouragement. At some point we have to stop in our tracks, stomp our feet, and say, "I won't take this anymore! I refuse to believe I am nothing, because Jesus says I am something! Though the enemy tells me I'll surely fail, God says He will not fail me!" This is the kind of tough stance I am talking about.

When the enemy tries to hurl his lies at you—even though they are wrapped in kernels of truth—do not break rank and try to defend yourself. Stand strong and be tough against the lies of the enemy. Don't wonder over or ponder the wretched things he says to you. His voice is always condemning, always betraying, and always making you wonder if God is who He says He is.

Be tough against his lies and assaults. Don't rehash fears or worry about failures. Don't allow yourself to be singled out when the enemy is attacking you. Not here. Not now. Stay in rank with the rest of us. You have a host of heaven and the multitudes of believers on your side. This is not to say you're perfect or even blameless. But those areas are reserved for the loving intervention and discipline of Almighty God. Take a firm stand against the lies of the enemy.

4. The fight for TENDERNESS (BOWS): "Humble yourselves, therefore, under God's mighty hand, that he may lift you up in due time" (1 Peter 5:6). In the Gospels, Jesus compares the Kingdom of God to a field where a farmer sowed good seed, but while he slept, an enemy came and sowed bad seed. Side by side, wheat and tares grew up together. One was the real deal; the other was just pretending to be.

A man once asked me, "Do you know how farmers tell the difference between wheat and tares, since from a distance they look so much alike?"

"No. Please tell me!" I replied.

He barely let me finish, he was so excited. "When the wind blows, the wheat *bows* down."

Wow. I was speechless. The tares are apparently rigid and unbending. Kind of reminds you of the religious Pharisee, no? When God breathes on us and we know He is speaking to us, we are to be flexible in His hands; not rigid and stiff. We are to bow like the wheat. And like Jesus.

Jesus didn't just act humble; He *was* humility.

> Your attitude should be the same as that of Christ Jesus: Who, being in very nature God, did not consider equality with God something to be grasped, but made himself nothing, taking the very nature of a servant, being made in human likeness. (Philippians 2:5–7)

Think about that statement for a moment: *He did not consider equality with God a thing to be grasped.* Jesus was equal with God, but didn't consider this equality as something to use for His advantage or to impress others. He didn't throw His weight around, because He knew who He was. He entrusted Himself to the Father because He trusted the Father. He was tough against the enemy and humble before the God of heaven.

The uncommon woman continually grows in her understanding of her place before God. She stands strong against the lies of the enemy, but in the presence of God, her knees buckle. She regularly meditates on certain passages of Scripture because they take her breath away. She listens to God's voice, and most of the time, she's quick to obey. She humbly responds to God's dealings with her because she knows how much she needs Him.

She knows that she is capable of stumbling in a thousand different ways and yet relishes the idea that God is on her side. She's nothing without Him and everything to Him, and that very thought makes her feel especially safe.

Martin Luther wrote, "God created the world out of nothing, and as long as we are nothing, He can make something out of us."[5]

The battlegrounds beneath our feet are the places in our lives where we refuse to humbly bow before the Lord so that He might have His way. Maybe it's your finances; God wants you to tithe, and you don't think you have the money. Maybe it's your frantic schedule; God wants you to rest, do less, and do it better; and you're afraid to disappoint others. Maybe you are white-knuckle-parenting your kids because you're motivated by fear; God wants you to trust Him and you want Him to trust *you*. We all have our places where we stand rigid.

The fight for us is the fight against our own stubborn willfulness and hardness of heart. It's the thing that keeps us from bowing, worshiping, and humbly obeying when it's difficult to do so. It's easy to trust God when the answers to our prayers come quickly, but it's tougher to do when we're not getting what we want from God. It's easy to praise Him when we've just received a bonus, but it's tougher to do when we wonder how we'll pay the bills. It's easy to obediently bow when we are praying for someone else's mess, but it's quite another thing when we have our own sins to reckon with.

The very act of keeping Christ at a safe distance (because of busyness, unforgiveness, distractions, and so on) only feeds our stubborn will and makes it stronger. Our carnal nature is empowered when we stay out of the presence of God. But when we refuse to let our "self-sins" rule, when we bring ourselves to the cross, and when we remember the basin, we see again the mercy and humility with which Jesus lived, and we are once again compelled to be more like Him.

When we grow comfortable in God's presence, we more easily trust Him to deal with our inconsistencies. When we believe that He has our best interests at heart, bowing before Him then becomes the most natural thing on earth. Just like breathing. "My hands have made both heaven and earth; they and everything in them are mine. I, the Lord, have spoken! I will bless those who have humble and contrite hearts, who tremble at my word" (Isaiah 66:2 NLT).

5. The fight to PERSEVERE: "So let's not allow ourselves to get fatigued doing good. At the right time we will harvest a good crop if we don't give up, or quit" (Galatians 6:9 THE MESSAGE). If you've read my other books or heard me speak, you know that I've

had some significant battles with health issues. My dad once told me that I remind him of the Wilma Flintstone bop bag he got me for Christmas one year. You knock her down; she pops back up. You knock her down again; she pops back up again. I've been knocked down a number of times, but I just don't like it down there.

A number of years ago, I released a book titled *Balance That Works When Life Doesn't*. Even though I'd had a number of other things published prior to the balance book, this contract was a real turning point for me. I was excited to get *Balance* into the hands of those who would benefit from it.

The month *Balance* released, I was scheduled to speak at a women's retreat in the beautiful mountains of Idaho. Sitting in the front row with my head bowed, I asked God to prepare my heart that I might be able to reliably convey His heart. I said "Amen" and prepared to walk up on stage. As soon as I looked up, the room started spinning. Thus began for me about a six-month battle with vertigo. It came and barely went, but even when the symptoms waned a bit, I was still off balance. Hmmm. Define irony: Release a book on balance and lose your balance, all in the same month.

This was devastating to me. I could barely get through my days because I was sick with dizziness. When I rolled over in bed at night, things spun so fast that if not for my oak tree of a husband, I would have ended up on the floor, night after night.

I kept all of my speaking engagements, but I literally had to be walked up to the podium on several occasions.

In the morning I would come down for my quiet time and try to pray. I opened my Bible only to watch the words whiz by me like cars zipping down the express lane. I would close my Bible, grit my teeth, and declare, "The enemy will not steal this time from me even if I can't read the Bible right now! I will pray what I know and believe what God says!" Then I would proceed to pray all of the Scripture I had memorized and had hidden in my heart.

During the sleepless nights, I was frustrated, sad, mad, and completely at a loss. Why did God allow such a big breakthrough in my writing only to allow this to happen? In a day when authors are expected to be heavily active in marketing their books, there was very little I could do.

And yet every time I showed up for my out-of-kilter quiet time, I could hear the faint whisper across my heart. *Keep going. Keep declaring. Keep believing. There's a reward on the other side of this for you. Persevere and do not give up. I have great things ahead for you.* And I knew it was true.

When the dizziness finally left me, something marvelous happened. In came a divine clarity in my thoughts, my purpose, and my prayers. New ministry doors opened up for me, and I had a fresh fire in my soul. And in a divine and profound way, I understood that in all things, God gets to decide how my life goes, and in every season, I will believe Him to be big in my midst.

Over and over again, the Bible tells us that He rewards those who seek after Him. He works for those who wait for Him. He blesses those who are willing to persevere. Take inventory of your life right now. Is there an area where you are growing faint or losing your steam?

You might be just steps away from your breakthrough! Don't let the enemy convince you that it's too difficult! Ask God for a renewed sense of vigor and passion and purpose. Ask Him to give you a glimpse of your breakthrough, and then persevere, putting one step in front of the other, and go on to possess your next place of promise.

> *Many who drop out of ministry are sufficiently gifted, but have large areas of life floating free from the Holy Spirit's control.*[6]
>
> J. OSWALD SANDERS

Always, when the Lord leads us on a path overgrown with thickets and dead branches, it's because there is a healing pool on the other side. Persevere, my friend, because the blessing always far outweighs the battle.

"Perseverance must finish its work so that you may be mature and complete, not lacking anything" (James 1:4).

Precious Lord,
I need You every hour. Help me to know when to stand strong and when to bow low. May my discernment be sharp that I might quickly put the enemy's insults under my feet. May my heart be so humble that I am quick to bow and glorify Your name. Grant me vision and perseverance that I may find strength in the hard times. And when I'm tempted not to forgive, remind me once again what You've done for me. I want to give You a great return on Your investment in me. Call me higher, Lord. Amen.

Declaration:
I declare that I am a humble, faithful follower of Christ! I am quick to hear and quick to obey. I forgive those who come against me, and I trust God to vindicate me. I know that as I humble myself before the Lord, He will lift me up in due time. I have all of the spiritual energy I need to persevere because God is with me every step of the way. Victory is mine as I march forward to the next place God has for me!

1. Read Psalm 119:1–3 and rewrite each of the verses in this passage in a declarative, personalized way that is specific to your life (e.g., *I will stay on God's path by avoiding . . .*).

2. Read Luke 14:7–11 and pause for a moment. Prayerfully ask the Lord to reveal to you anything you've done lately to "take the seat of honor." Take a moment to repent and then thank the Lord for His great love for you.

3. Read Colossians 3:12–15 and notice how the first part of verse 12 makes a statement about who you are. Based on this verse, who are you? Write it down, followed by a prayer thanking God for this truth.

4. Look at the second part of verse 12. As an uncommon woman, how are you supposed to clothe yourself? Write it down and feel free to expand on these a bit.

5. Read verse 13 and in your own words, describe the difference between "bear with" and "forgive." How are you doing in this area?

6. In verses 14 and 15, you are called to "put on . . . ", "let . . . ", and "be . . . ". Fill in those blanks and then write some concrete examples of how you can apply these in your own life.

7. Write down what you're thankful for.

the uncommon
woman
embraces
a different
perspective

The expression of God's unconditional
love always produces a miracle.[1]
∿MICHAEL YOUSSEF

So we have stopped evaluating others from a
human point of view. At one time we thought
of Christ merely from a human point of view.
How differently we know him now!
∿2 CORINTHIANS 5:16 NLT

understands
that love *sees*
and love covers

Once upon a time there was a woman who was a terrible house-keeper. Like the old woman who lived in the shoe, she had lots of children and didn't know what to do. She had more dirty laundry than not, and more dirty dishes than clean. Her house was cluttered with stacks of papers, dirty toys, and old books. She would choose reading over cleaning any day of the week. Her kids were disheveled but seemed happy to spend time with their mom. She loved God, but for the life of her, she couldn't present well.

One day a crisis struck her family, and she was suddenly widowed. Paralyzed with fear, this young mom stood in the middle of her messy living room, stared out her dirty window, and began to cry.

Within hours her house was filled with well-meaning friends from church. Some started upstairs, others started down. Together they worked hard to clean up her place, stock up a few meals, and help with the kids.

Don't you just love the church? I do too. Really.

But what happened next makes me so very sad. This grieving, young widow suddenly became the topic of conversation. At church over cookies and coffee things were said like, "I can't believe how unorganized she is." And, "*I* could never live like that." And, "Uh, are we really *helping* her by helping her? Or is that what you call enabling?" One woman who didn't make it out to the house asked, "What do you mean? What was it like?" Though she didn't help with the cleaning, she certainly got an earful about the mess.

Because of the crisis in her home, the young widow's weaknesses were laid bare for all to see. In her moment of vulnerability when she really needed to be protected, she was exposed.

⁂

To some who were confident of their own righteousness and looked down on everybody else, Jesus told this parable: "Two men went up to the temple to pray, one a Pharisee and the other a tax collector. The Pharisee stood up and prayed about himself: 'God, I thank you that I am not like other men—robbers, evildoers, adulterers—or even like this tax collector. I fast twice a week and give a tenth of all I get.' But the tax collector stood at a distance. He would not even look up to heaven, but beat his breast and said, 'God, have mercy on me, a sinner.' I tell you that this man, rather than the other, went home justified before God. For everyone who exalts himself will be humbled, and he who humbles himself will be exalted. (Luke 18:9–14)

Love Sees . . .

Many years ago, I was sick with Lyme disease and our house was falling apart. I felt like a debt to society and especially to my family—I could do nothing for them except listen to how their day went and pray for them. We were flat broke. My life seemed like it was at a dead end without much hope for restoration.

And still, I hoped. I hoped with all my heart. Anticipation rose up within me at the thought of being healed and restored. Amidst my mess of a life, I finally found a hope that my life would someday be marked by blessing and not by crisis. When I shared my hopes and dreams, an arrogant woman patted me on the head and said condescendingly, "Well, I believe, *you* believe that will happen." Her life looked perfect, mine looked pathetic. Maybe she really knew, and maybe I was the fool.

> But God chose the foolish things of the world to shame the wise;
> God chose the weak things of the world to shame the strong.
> (1 Corinthians 1:27)

God *did* heal and restore me. He did so beyond my wildest dreams. He answered my prayers, strengthened my faith, and made me more like Him! I was so thankful I hadn't ever lost that little seed of faith and hope that He would make things new for me once again.

Years later I heard how this person had stumbled into her own pile of dirt. And do you know what my first thoughts were? My instinctive reactions were not of sadness, compassion, or even empathy for her. *I was glad that she finally got what was coming to her.* How quickly I had manifested the Pharisee I loathed!

The Holy Spirit's conviction was so strong in me that I was sickened by the dueling natures within my own heart. As soon as I detected the grotesque pride that had poisoned my mind, I was bowing before the Lord, begging for mercy for my wretched soul.

I knew with all my heart that I had no business embracing any posture other than gratitude and humility. I was an orphan, and He had adopted me.

I used to think there was a remarkable contrast between the tax collector and the Pharisee who stood before the Lord, proclaiming the condition of their hearts. But as I have messed up in my own life, I have realized how closely linked they actually are. In fact, sometimes they can represent *the same person*.

Jesus said that the pure in heart are blessed, because they will see God (see Matthew 5:8). When we earnestly pursue purity in our own thoughts and hearts, we will acquire a supernatural ability to *see* others the way Jesus sees them. It won't matter if they move fast and you move slowly—if you guard your heart when you think of them, you'll get a front-row seat to *see* God's divine love work in them, and you'll be nourished as you watch their life's story unfold.

On the other hand, when our hearts are muddied with self-righteousness and pettiness against someone, we don't *get* to see what God is doing in and through them. Our eyes are blinded to the blessings in them because we've lost the right to see into their lives. God won't let us in on the precious treasure of their strengths because, right now, we're mishandling their weaknesses.

God will not take their treasures and toss them on the ground for us to grind under our feet. The more we allow critical and catty thoughts to swirl around in our brain, the more blinded we become. And the more blinded we become, the more we miss all of the beautiful things God is doing in our world.

The common woman thinks nothing of casually dismissing another woman in her moment of weakness. The enemy loves it when this happens. He is thrilled when we attack our own because we accomplish his purposes and we discredit ourselves in the process.

As I have suffered from the pain that has both come at me and come from me, I've come to realize something very important: *Christ's work in all of us is sacred*. Your process, my process, messy as it is sometimes, is holy ground.

The highs and lows of our journey mean something to God. And when I casually step all over your holy ground as if it's nothing but dirt and sand, I become blinded by my own ignorance. In that very moment you are the one holding the pearls, and I have become the swine (sad to say). Let's look at the verse:

"Do not give dogs what is sacred; do not throw your pearls to pigs. If you do, they may trample them under their feet, and then turn and tear you to pieces" (Matthew 7:6).

True love sees. And if she can't see, she presses in until she does. She prays, she seeks, she asks, and she believes that every person is made in the image of God. What a treasure is hidden in you! Open any one of us up and you'll find gems, jewels, and treasures galore. How do we unlock the treasure in those we don't necessarily understand? We receive them just as they are. We love them.

Not that we are supposed to be best friends with everybody; obviously not. We don't even have to trust everybody. In fact, we shouldn't. But we can still love them. My paraphrase of Matthew 10:41 is this: When we receive another righteous sister in the Lord with the love of Christ, we get to be on the receiving end of all of the treasures buried within her. Our eyes are opened to her inner beauty, and though this is not our goal, we get to benefit from all that's good about her. We give her love; we receive her blessing. What a wonderful concept.

Greater still is that when we stand shoulder to shoulder with our arms linked, the enemy will have a hard time knowing where I end and you begin. Then, suddenly, my victory becomes your victory. My fruit becomes your fruit. And when we stand together, Christ commands a blessing.

> How wonderful, how beautiful, when brothers and sisters get along! Yes, that's where God commands the blessing, ordains eternal life. (Psalm 133:1, 3 THE MESSAGE)

So why *do* we gossip and have a tendency to denigrate people who struggle with things that we don't? Furthermore, when *we* are on the receiving end of someone else's wrong perspective, is it possible to be deeply hurt by them and still come through it stronger and more pure than ever? (We'll answer these questions in the next chapter.) In a world full of fallen people—ourselves at the forefront—how do we walk the way Jesus did? Amidst the conflict and the pettiness, is it possible to see the world through His eyes?

Friends will betray us and colleagues will treat us unjustly. What are we supposed to do with that? What's more, how should we deal with those character traits in others that just make us want to turn and run? If we are honest with ourselves, we admit that we sometimes write people off because they are too much work. I know I have at times kept a safe distance from abrasive people because I've not been fond of getting scraped.

But as I look deeply at Jesus' example of humbly washing feet, I find myself thoroughly convicted over that attitude. There was hardly a more abased role He could have embraced. By this time, the disciples were getting used to Jesus' unconventional ways . . . but what was God's Son doing wrapped in a servant's apron and carrying a grimy bowl?

Let's peek in at the exchange between Peter and Jesus:

[After Jesus] wrapped a towel around his waist . . . he poured water into a basin and began to wash his disciples' feet, drying them with the towel that was wrapped around him. He came to Simon Peter, who said to him, "Lord, are you going to wash my feet?" Jesus replied, "You do not realize now what I am doing, but later you will understand." "No," said Peter, "you shall never wash my feet." Jesus answered, "Unless I wash you, you have no part with me." "Then, Lord," Simon Peter replied, "not just my feet but my hands and my head as well!" Jesus answered, "A person who has had a bath needs only to wash his feet; his whole body is clean. And you are clean." (John 13:4–10)

When a person is in Christ, she is a *new creation*. Old things have passed away, and all things are new. When Jesus spoke to Peter about those who have had a bath, He was referring to His children—to us. Remember, when we receive Christ, our identity is secure, and no person, position, or opinion can ever change that! Since that's true, the world doesn't get to determine our worth. Furthermore, we have no business summing up another's worth based on our worldly perception of her.

The verse at the beginning of this chapter says it all: "From now on we regard *no one* from a worldly point of view" (2 Corinthians 5:16). We need a new perspective. We need eyes to *see through* the façade, the pain, and the seemingly fatal flaws in others that make us want to step away from them. With God's help uncommon women everywhere can rise above their natural tendencies toward pettiness and insecurity and see other women as Christ sees them: as ones who have a heart, a destiny, and a pile of fears and insecurities that need to be redeemed. Just like the rest of us.

If you struggle with seeing yourself as Christ sees you, try this once. Visualize yourself wrapped in a white robe embroidered with *His* initials that rest upon your heart. Wrapped around you is a robe of righteousness that *covers* you (and all of your personality lumps and bumps) and says you've had a bath (love covers a multitude of sins)! You've been washed clean! Jesus has got you covered. Your identity has been established and you have been purified in Christ. Love sees. And Jesus *loves* what He sees in you.

Instead of seeing ourselves (and others) as a sum of flaws and attributes, we must constantly *look for* and see before us beautiful creations, designed for a marvelous purpose. Because that's what we are. That's *who* we are.

Love Covers . . .

We have all been hit with the flu at least once in our lives; close your eyes and recall with me how you looked. Do you remember how your hair was jacked up on one side and how rancid your breath was? How about the wrinkled, damp pajamas that clung to your feverish body and that by then should have been changed and replaced . . . several times over? Since your world had been reduced to a bucket and a toilet bowl, you couldn't even imagine what the rest of the house looked like . . . nor did you care. Is it coming back to you now?

You really know you've been sick when you get your first look in the mirror after a few days in bed . . . and instead of gasping at the sight of yourself, you just push a hunk of hair back in place and shrug your shoulders. If only you could blow into your thumb to reinflate your droopy eyes and bring them back up to the surface of your face!

Personally, after spending a night in the bathroom with my head in the bowl, I start to feel more than a little disgusting. The days of being showered and groomed seem eons ago. A mental picture of myself bouncing through my days with energy and zeal seems almost uncapturable.

However, the flu usually only lasts for a short while, and then recovery comes. How quickly we forget our wretched time by the toilet.

We also have "flu seasons" in our lives. Everyone has a time in their lives when they don't look as put together as they would like. Specifically, the Lord allows His children to walk through incredible pain, and it is an agonizingly vulnerable thing for the world to see us this way.

Jesus promised us that we would have many trials in this short life. When others struggle with the things we have recently come through, we normally have grace for them. For instance, when my husband had cancer, some of the people who were the most helpful to him were the ones who had walked that same path.

Unfortunately, we have a harder time extending grace toward those who struggle with areas that happen to be our areas of strength. If we're good with money, we tend to look down on the one who doesn't have the savvy instinct that we possess. If we're generally healthy, we feel sure that the chronically ill must be doing something wrong.

If we're honest here, most of us at some time or other feel subtly proud of our strengths when we're around a weakling. For the most part, we try not to judge them, but we wonder why they can't get it together. (Now, I know this isn't always the case. There are some precious, godly people who have the maturity and tenderness to enter in and minister to others in most any area without a hint of judgment. God bless them.)

It is interesting, though, to note how subtly we take ownership of and credit for our areas of strength. If we aren't careful, we will come to believe that these strengths *define* us. We start to trust in the gifts instead of the Giver. It is like climbing off the Vine and dangling on our own branch. What a dangerous thing to do.

When our lives are sick with the spiritual flu, we feel broken and ashamed as we helplessly watch our weaknesses come to the surface. It is normal to want to hide and pretend. These are the times when we learn the most about ourselves, and we have learned well if during them we find ourselves on our faces before God, calling out for Him to carry us through. We are transient creatures, but we are carried by God.

There are also the seasons, though, when it appears that the Lord has given us a break from having to look so deeply at ourselves. Life doesn't feel so difficult and we are able to coast just a bit. We loosen our grip, believe in ourselves a little too much, and as a result, we put ourselves at risk of either falling into sin . . . or of becoming a Pharisee.

When we're healthy and generally thriving, we forget how

disgusting we looked as we hung over the commode. But we *must* remember how we looked if we have any hope of being a reliable messenger (see Proverbs 13:17). Hanging on to the maxim "There but for the grace of God go I" is the first step in moving toward the kind of maturity and love that covers a multitude of sins. Humble love is the *only* kind of love.

When we encounter someone who is living through her own flu season, we remember what we looked like when life was messy, and we step up or stoop down, whichever is required; but our goal is to love her and cover her, even if her struggle is something we cannot comprehend.

If in our fullness and health we can humbly come alongside someone who is sick or hurting, we will be serving as Jesus did. If we struggle with being the judgmental type, then until we come to terms with the truth about ourselves, we must stay far away from the struggling person, lest we do more harm than good. But if we can truly remember where we came from, and who we would be without Jesus . . . we might be the person that the Lord uses to wash the wounded one's feet and nurse her back to health. And what we do for her, we do for Him. An honor indeed.

Over and over Jesus lived the example of getting dirty while remaining pure. In other words, He walked into the disarray of other people's lives and left them better than He found them. He served people who couldn't get it together, and yet He always loved. If anybody had the right to breathe a critical sigh, our perfect Savior did. But He didn't do that to the messy and the exposed. He loved them. He covered them. And He stood in the gap for them. He got His hands grimy, yet kept His heart pure.

"There is a moment of truth for everyone," a friend once shared. "People make that conscious choice in their minds when they are faced with the irritating flaws in others: 'Will I step away and judge them or will I draw nearer and serve them?' "[2] So much hinges on that moment of truth.

We need each other. Great things happen when we support one another in our times of need. There's power in numbers and God blesses it when we come together for the right reasons. The truth is, though, that for many of us, our times of need reveal dirty messes we'd just as soon sweep under the rug. And since many of us have had our dirty rugs shaken for all to see (and those who saw were not very gracious), we would much rather handle our problems alone.

This question begs an answer from each of us: Can we be faithful with other people's messes? Do we know what it means to cover someone because this is the same kindness Christ has extended to us?

Consider Noah. He was a man God recognized above all others. He had a righteous heart and a desire to follow God. The Lord asked him to do mind-boggling things—things that nowadays could have been interpreted as grounds for some kind of diagnosis—and yet over and over the Bible states that Noah did *exactly* what the Lord asked him to do. He had grit. He took risks. He followed God.

But then one night as he spent time in his vineyard, he imbibed too much and got sloppy drunk—and there is great speculation as to why he took off his clothes and passed out naked. This was not Noah's finest hour . . . in fact, it was just the opposite. It was his time of "hanging over the commode." My heart ached for him as I read his story in the book of Genesis.

It seems that Noah's son Ham was the first one to see his father completely sloshed and exposed. Do you know what he did with that information? *He ran and told. . . .* How often do we do that? Sometimes we hear something that we are just dying to tell someone. It may be information that fills in the gaps of some things we had been wondering about. It's going to get out anyway . . . right?

Wrong. The more we follow the impulse to "run and tell," the more calloused our feet become to the damage we are doing. The call of the uncommon woman goes against this grain. Her path is an altogether different one. Read this beautiful verse from Proverbs: "(She) who covers over an offense promotes love, but whoever repeats the matter separates close friends" (17:9).

Maybe you are wondering, "Does 'cover each other' mean we are supposed to sweep our sinful dysfunctions under the rug?" Absolutely not. But isn't it safe to say that the majority of the run-and-tell information that we share is gossip—no matter how you slice it? C. S. Lewis wisely wrote these wonderful words:

> Abstain from all thinking about other people's faults, unless your duties as a teacher or parent make it necessary to think about them. Whenever the thoughts come unnecessarily into one's mind, why not simply shove them away? And think of one's own faults instead? For there, with God's help, one can do something. Of all the awkward people in your house or job there is only one whom you can improve very much. That is the practical end at which to begin. And really, we'd better. The job has to be tackled some day: and every day we put it off will make it harder to begin.[3]

Scripture also gives us some direction on how to deal with another's sin:

> Dear brothers and sisters, if another believer is overcome by some sin, you who are godly should gently and humbly help that person back onto the right path. And be careful not to fall into the same temptation yourself. Share each other's burdens, and in this way obey the law of Christ. If you think you are too important to help someone in need, you are only fooling yourself. You are not that important. (Galatians 6:1–3 NLT)

Did you know that you can build a case against anybody? Do you know that the devil accuses us day and night? We would do well to remember that some women who are currently the delicious topic of conversation are actually in their refining time. God is getting ready to promote them. We will be held accountable for how we speak about the Lord's anointed, whether she is hiding in a cave or crawling through a valley.

Our time would be much better served as God's precious, uncommon women if we were to pour our energy, our passion, and our words into prayers for people and the things we notice about them.

Think about it. Imagine if you knew Beth Moore back when she was going through the fire before her ministry exploded onto the scenes, and instead of being jealous of her beauty and charm, you interceded for her as a sister in the Lord. Right now you would be a wealthy benefactor of the victory and the fruit that is bursting from her life and ministry. Your spiritual investment would be multiplied many times over.

You know, Noah had two other sons, and they handled his situation quite differently. Read on:

> Shem and Japheth took a garment and laid it across their shoulders; then they walked in backward and covered their father's nakedness. (Genesis 9:23)

They covered their father's nakedness

Shem and Japheth were blessed because they made the choice that the news of Noah's dirt—Noah's sick moment—would stop with them. Read the story and be amazed by the incredible ripple effect because of the decision to honor and the decision to dishonor. Shem, Japheth, and their families were greatly blessed by their father for that single act. They received a righteous man's reward. Love saw and love covered. And blessings were passed down as a result. "A woman's wisdom gives her patience; it is to her glory to overlook an offense" (see Proverbs 19:11).

◦◦

As I read the verse at the beginning of the chapter, I can almost picture the far-off look in Paul's eyes as he wrote those words. "So we have stopped evaluating others from a human point of view. At one time we thought of Christ merely from a human point of view. How differently we know him now!" (2 Corinthians 5:16 NLT) Jesus walked with, hung with, and loved the most humble and the most needy people on the planet. This was God in the dirt. Jesus' actions, at every turn, revealed God's heart for us. He was real, He was present; He was full of power and rich in understanding. Though He was wrapped in skin and muscle and bone and tendon, He was still God. Though His feet shuffled through the dirt, His perspective always came from heaven. Amazing love.

> *Things human must be known to be loved; things divine must be loved to be known.*
> BLAISE PASCAL

Precious Lord,
I'm amazed by You. My righteousness amounts to a pile of filthy rags, and yet when You look at me, I'm wearing a royal robe. I need You every day and I have You every moment. Please, Lord, give me eyes to see, ears to hear, and a heart to do Your will. Grant me a willingness to love the unlovable. Help me remember that pride goes before a fall and humility precedes honor. Grant me the capacity to cover those who are walking through a vulnerable time. May there be such integrity in my words that anyone and everyone will

feel safe in my presence; just as I feel safe in Yours.
What a treasure You are to me, Lord. Lead me on.
Amen.

Declaration:
In Jesus' Name I declare that I walk in the Spirit and
do not gratify the desires of the flesh! God opens
my mouth with skillful and godly wisdom; He puts
kindness in my words. I am daily growing in my capacity to love the unlovely. I refuse gossip and pettiness because I refuse to be used by the enemy. I will
instead speak words of power, and life, and healing.
I see the treasure in others even when no one else
does. Daily the Lord opens doors for me that I
might be a blessing to others. I embrace my identity
in Christ, and His message of reconciliation flows
consistently through me!

what about you?

1. Read 2 Corinthians 5:14–16 and consider these three
   things: Who did He die for? Who are we supposed
   to live for? How are we supposed to view others?
   Answer these questions and then give a personal example of how you can live for Him (and love because of Him) instead of going your own way.

2. Read 2 Corinthians 5:17–19 and ponder this passage

for a moment. It's powerful. Rewrite these three verses in your own words. You've been commissioned with a high calling indeed! It's interesting that woven into these verses is a reminder to keep your perspective when carrying out this call. How are we to view others as we pursue this ministry of reconciliation?

3. Read 2 Corinthians 5:20–21, and in light of the basin and the cross, think about the way Jesus lived. He became the servant and the sacrifice that we might become righteousness and royalty. Describe how that makes you feel.

4. Read Proverbs 28:13, and notice something important here. We expose our own sin, but we cover in love the sins of another (notice I'm not saying cover up the sins of another). It's tempting to "cover our own sin" by pointing to or exposing someone else's foibles. Write your thoughts on this verse and the ways we tend to mishandle information.

5. Read this verse: "Unfailing love and faithfulness make atonement for sin. By fearing the Lord, people avoid evil" (Proverbs 16:6 NLT). How can an uncommon woman live out this verse? Write down your thoughts by rewriting this verse in a paragraph, paraphrased form.

6. Read Proverbs 17:9. Using this verse as a guideline, write a prayerful plea asking God to make you more like Him.

Just because something
makes sense, doesn't mean it's true.
&LUKE LARSON (10TH GRADER)

Their eyes are blinded, their hearts are
hardened, so that they wouldn't see with their
eyes and perceive with their hearts, and
turn to me, God, so I could heal them.
&JOHN 12:40 THE MESSAGE

chapter six

values truth
over perception

A number of years ago, a good friend of mine was struggling through feelings of despair and depression. She asked a couple of friends to meet her for a time of prayer. We sat on the living room floor and listened as she shared about her doubts and fears.

She was from a prominent, accomplished family. They were all well educated and well-to-do. She was a stay-at-home mom. She had a fierce love for Jesus, her friends, and her family. And yet, her heart was in deep despair.

As we gathered around her and rested our hands on her shoulders, we asked the Holy Spirit to fill our hearts and guide our time of prayer. With my eyes closed, I sought the Lord on behalf of my friend. Instantly a picture flashed across my mind.

I saw my friend standing alone covered in banners; labels given to her by the enemy of her soul. These draped banners said things like "Unlovely," "Not Capable," "Not Accomplished," "Overly Emotional," "Never Enough," "Not Smart," and more. With her head low and her eyes on the floor, I pictured my friend slumped beneath the lying banners that hung like heavy chains.

Hanging out of her reach were bright banners that said things like "Smart," "Person of Position," "Accomplished," "Educated," "Respected," and so on. She was bound by the lies of her labels, and desperately longed for the more impressive banners.

As I relayed this word picture, my friend's eyes welled up with tears. Her lips quivered and she wiped her eyes. She nodded and explained how accurately this picture described her feelings. More tears came, and this time we encouraged her not to hold anything back, but to be honest about everything she was feeling and thinking. She sobbed; we held her, and together we went before the Lord.

Before we prayed, we had a wonderful discussion about Jesus. We were all amazed by the way He came to earth, by the way He lived His life . . . and by the way He died. *Everything* He did blew the doors off of pretense and position. The world waited for a mighty and majestic king to enter the scene with grandeur and pageantry. Christ came into the world through the womb of a teenage girl. He was born in a place where animals live. At every turn, Jesus put the value on the things that mattered instead of the things of appearance. Jesus was *never* impressed by anyone's position, only by the condition of one's heart.

Jesus came to destroy the evil hierarchy that exists in our world. The Bible says that He resists and distances Himself from the proud, but He gives grace to the humble. He draws near to and confides in those who love and fear Him. He confronts those who are impressed only with themselves.

Consequently, the banners of title and position are *not* the solutions for someone burdened by labels accumulated from past hurts. They are merely substitutes for the true identity that Jesus offers. Covering up insecurities with accomplishments never turns lies into truths.

What's wonderful is that Jesus came to take off the demeaning dunce caps that have been piled on our heads. He gladly peels off the scarlet letters that have been pinned all over us. Whatever we have been through, whatever we have done, whatever others say about us, Jesus can forgive it, heal it, rebuild it, and redeem it! He makes all things new.

Jesus came to set the captives free, give sight to the blind, and strengthen the weak. *Nothing's* too hard for Him. There is no past He can't restore, no lie He can't erase, and no offense He can't make right. He takes the stones that have injured us and turns them into jewels fit for a crown.

He is our Redeemer, our Friend, and our Savior. He makes all things bright and beautiful. All of nature knows Him; the angels revere Him, and the devil fears Him. He is in our corner, on our side, and in our hearts. He is the first and the last, the beginning and the end. If God is for us, who can be against us?

Psalm 27:1 says, "The Lord is my light and my salvation—whom shall I fear? The Lord is the stronghold of my life—of whom shall I be afraid?" He is our Light . . . He'll show us the way. He is our salvation . . . our eternity is secured. He is the stronghold where we can abide and be safe from the assaults of the enemy. No one can make us inferior because Jesus has made us whole. We can look to Him for all that we need. He is more than able. Praise the Lord!

As my friends and I sat on the floor discussing the living power that Jesus offers, our excitement escalated. We surrounded our friend and prayerfully discredited the labels the enemy had given her. We told her to picture each banner coming off as she named it and refuted its lie. And she did. One at a time. Every single one.

She sobbed as she freely released the things she thought had defined her. After the lies were exposed and gone, our friend was ready to hear the truth. And we poured it over her like a living stream of water. As if she were standing in a welcomed spring rain after the storm, our sweet friend opened her hands and looked up, not wanting to miss a drop. Slowly and gradually, her smile lines returned. Her tear-filled eyes spilled with joy. And she was cleansed from the inside out.

We watched in awe the unfolding of this promise: *God's precious and powerful truth sets—us—free*—not accomplishments, not money, not impressive associations, not a respectable position, not a polished presentation, or even the world's perception of us. Only *our acceptance* of God's divine love and *our belief* in His ability to restore will set us free and make us into the uncommon women we were always meant to be. When saving face is replaced by saving grace, everything changes.

⊸⊚⊶

> Now before the Passover Feast began, Jesus knew (was fully aware) that the time had come for Him to leave this world and return to the Father. And as He had loved those who were His own in the world, He loved them to the last and to the highest degree. (John 13:1 AMP)

For the Jews, Passover represented the beginning of a new nation—their nation. Just before Moses had led them out of Egypt, the Lord had instituted the Passover celebration as both a memorial and a foretelling of *His* mighty deliverance.

Many generations later, in Jesus' day, the time of Passover had come, and many celebrations were once again taking place. I can imagine the hordes of pilgrims shuffling along the dirt roads around Jerusalem making their way to the temple. This was the place to be. I wonder how many people pressed through the crowds just to catch a glimpse of the power brokers of their day (the priests and religious rulers), who in turn looked down upon the common folk. Even back then, perception was paramount.

But just across the way in an upper room of a borrowed home, something far more significant was coming about. The church was being born.

God was in town, but He wasn't in the middle of the pomp and the circumstance. He wasn't with the "important" religious leaders of that day. He was reclining with a group of men who had dirty feet. He knew His time on earth was drawing to a close, and He was about to teach those who would listen, how *He* wanted His church to function.

Jesus was disgusted by self-important posturing, and passionate about love. He detested shallow arrogance but embraced humility and holiness. He was toughest on the prideful and most tender with the grimy sinner who knew she was a grimy sinner. He spent time with the vagabond and the prostitute, the impulsive and the marginalized, because they all had this in common: they knew they needed Him.

⌒ ⊚ ⊚

One of the golden calves in our day is the idol of image and perception. People with no talent are paid millions simply because the masses perceive them to be someone of importance. Stellar musicians go unnoticed because they don't portray an image that sells. Average musicians become overnight successes because marketing gurus turn them into a caricature that fascinates us.

Much of what we see is not exactly how it is. In other words, just because someone appears to be at the top of their game doesn't mean they are. And just because someone appears to be useless doesn't mean they are.

In this image-driven world, just how are we supposed to discern the truth? In a postmodern culture that's made truth a negotiable, organic, fluid, optional item, why is it essential for the uncommon woman to defy the norm and stake her life upon truth? What *is* truth, exactly?

Want the truth? It's Jesus. He is the exact representation of Almighty God. Our heavenly Father is scandalously humble, abundantly loving, and purposely forgiving. He means what He says. He carries out His word. And He doesn't need us, though He loves the idea of having us on this journey with Him. He loved us first. And if we choose to walk away, it will be our loss indeed.

The prisoner, the pauper, and the prince approach Him on the same day and He loves them all, whether they understand Him or not. Our Creator God is the source of all things—and so—*the truth is whatever He says it is.* And even though we live in a day when many disagree with Him, He's still right.

- ❖ *The truth of God's Word forgives our sin—and we sin*—so we need this truth.
- ❖ *The truth of God's Word restores—and we get depleted*—so we need this truth.
- ❖ *The truth of God's Word convicts—and we are selfish*—so we need this truth.

When we're willing to look *past* the natural appearance of things in order to perceive God's superior reality, we will begin to see with eyes of faith and hope and love.

Instead of judging a woman who doesn't appear to be worshiping in church, we will pray for her sore back or her frozen shoulder. Before jumping to conclusions about a woman who has overlooked us, we will pray for her busy schedule. Rather than being critical of a woman who is always critical, we will lovingly ask God to heal her prickly heart.

When we're determined to *respond* to truth rather than *react* to someone's actions, we will less likely be ensnared by misassigned motives and wrong assessments.

When our perspective lines up with God's promises, we will walk about in freedom (see Psalm 119:45). The Bible says that these truths—His promises—are backed by the honor of His name. And to the believer, His name is our reason for being.

> I bow before your holy Temple as I worship. I will praise your name for your unfailing love and faithfulness; for your promises are backed by all the honor of your name. (Psalm 138:2 NLT)

If we are serious about becoming uncommon, we must give God full permission to invade our dark places with His powerful light. If we really want to make a difference in the world . . . we must allow God to make a difference in us. If we want to see others the way God sees them, we must see ourselves the way God sees us.

In order to gain a fresh perspective of our daily, moment-by-moment need for a mutual and thriving relationship with God, let's look again at the exchange between Peter and Jesus:

> [After Jesus] wrapped a towel around his waist . . . he poured water into a basin and began to wash his disciples' feet, drying them with the towel that was wrapped around him. He came to Simon Peter, who said to him, "Lord, are you going to wash my feet?" Jesus replied, "You do not realize now what I am doing, but later you will understand." "No," said Peter, "you shall never wash my feet." Jesus answered, "Unless I wash you, you have no part with me." "Then, Lord," Simon Peter replied, "not just my feet but my hands and my head as well!" Jesus answered, "A person who has had a bath needs only to wash his feet; his whole body is clean. And you are clean." (John 13:4–10)

Jesus told Peter that since he had a bath, he didn't need another one; he was already clean. So what did Jesus mean then when He told Peter, "Unless you have a bath, you have no part with me"?

Peter was clean. We are clean. Jesus established that. But He is also making an important point here. Even though we are clean because we are in Christ . . . we still have the problem of our dirty feet. This issue isn't with our identity but with our whereabouts. Our dirty feet do not speak of who we are, but rather of where we have been. We don't have to keep asking Jesus into our hearts to be our Savior. If Jesus is our Lord, we are saved.

However, even as we undergo the day-by-day process of sanctification, we live in a fallen world where sin abounds. Daily we do things, say things, and think things that we shouldn't. *This is the dirt that covers our feet.* Sometimes we go places we have no business going. Sometimes we watch things that pollute our souls. *This is the dirt that covers our feet.* Sometimes we embrace critical attitudes against others; and worse yet, we share our impassioned assessments with others. *This is the dirt that covers our feet.*

Just like Peter, there are places we have walked that have left us with dirty feet. Where have you been walking lately? Have you been lingering on the path of bitterness, lollygagging in an angry place, or shuffling around in self-pity? Have you spent too much time on the road to success and too little time in His presence? Have you been dancing around with fear, or hanging loosely with the unholy? Have you been sidestepping His voice? Examine where you've been. Jesus wants to move toward you with the towel and the basin.[1]

Sin separates us from God. Every time we walk through the filthy sin of this life, we need a fresh encounter with Jesus. We need to open our mouths, and with our own words tell Him the truth about what we've done. As humbling as it is, we need to put our soiled feet in His hands and confess to Him where we've been.

As we demean the importance of perception for the sake of

raw and naked truth, we position ourselves for renewal, refreshment, and for something better than the world's esteem. The uncommon path of humility and honesty always eventually leads to pools of blessing and a fresh outpouring of grace. On the other side of our humble confession waits forgiveness, intimacy, and a fresh anointing to live out our God-assigned destiny.

When we become brutally honest about the sin in our lives, Jesus is right there to forgive us, restore us, and stand us up on our clean feet again. Oh, the mercy of His love!

Picture Him on His knees, rugged fingers wrapped around your ankles, your toes. Look into His eyes and see the love that compelled Him to give His life. Imagine the wonder of watching the water become muddy as your feet become clean.

When our sin piles up, our identity is not up for grabs, but our fellowship with Jesus is. We are called to a vital, vested, active walk of faith. This calls for keeping short accounts with sin— both in confessing our sin and in forgiving the sins of others. It calls for a heart that is bent toward living like Jesus did. All pride goes out the door when we bring ourselves to the basin. As we look at the soiled water from our most recent escapades, we remember our constant, moment-by-moment need for Him.

Unless we get so real with God that we are regularly lifting up our filthy feet for Him to clean (along with our selfish, vindictive thoughts), we will miss the One-ness for which we were created.

As we look down at the water, opaque with blackness, there is no "trying" to be humble. We *are* humbled.

People *will* rub us the wrong way; some people will even devastate us. Jesus was devastated *to the point of death.* How do we deal with *this* kind of dirt? We remember the basin. We remember the muddy water from our own sin. We remember how it feels to pull clean feet from a dirty bowl. We strive to have a gentle heart toward others who need that kind of blessing. We accept God's mercy and endeavor to pass it on. We remember what Jesus did, and we embrace His call for us to do the same. We determine to *see* others as Christ sees us: Loved. Forgiven. Called. Chosen.

Part of becoming an uncommon woman is to radically believe the otherworldly truth about ourselves: that we are everything to God, and nothing without Him. And in our knowing, we step away from the need or desire to constantly manipulate other's perception of us. No longer will we need to serve our image or defend position. We will serve God, knowing *He* is the One who establishes us. He is the One who defends us.

Jesus knows us. He understands us. And He is the One who can do something about our lives. Since He is aware of our intentions (right, wrong, and otherwise), we are content to let that be enough. We determine to get off the common path of self-preservation and idealized impressions, and get on instead with life. We begin using our precious time and energy to fight the real fight of faith.

In his book *God Revealed*, Graham Cooke makes this delectable statement:

> A difference exists between our state and our standing. Our state is how we see ourselves. If we allow the enemy to lure us out of our safe place in Christ, we will see ourselves as weak, powerless, ineffective and worthless. But our standing is about who we are in Christ. When we learn to live in Christ, we take on His attributes. That's why I can write things like, "I'm brilliant." I know I'm brilliant because I stand in Christ and He's brilliant. There's something stupendous about being in Christ.[2]

Don't you just love that? I sure do! The more I pondered this author's statement, the more I grasped the truth behind it. All too often we get our perspective from our "state," which is comprised of our current circumstances and how we feel about them. And those things are *always* changing. We need to acknowledge when things are bad or when circumstances hurt us. Acknowledge, yes. Allow those things to cloud our view, no.

Since life can be unpredictable and people equally so, our "state" will be in constant fluctuation. What never changes though, is our place in Christ. Even if it doesn't feel true, we are seated with Christ. We have a holy place of position and authority because we belong to Him. When we enter a room, something in the spiritual climate changes because we are there. Our state is shifting sand. Our standing is solid ground.

Be real about your pain. But be right about your perspective. Always (even when it's difficult), embrace the truth of *who God is* and *what He says* about life and people and circumstances. If your circumstances say something different than God's Word, choose God's Word as your perspective.

> *In God's realm of infinite possibility and grace, the very thing that we think will disqualify us is the doorway through which the Father delivers His heart and affection for us. . . . His power is perfected in weakness because God's grace is always enough.*[3]
> GRAHAM COOKE

Stand on His promises and declare that you will see the goodness of the Lord in the land of the living (see Psalm 27:13)! Choose to believe the things He says over your limited view and understanding of how you perceive things to be. This will bring a little bit of heaven to earth.

"Now we see but a poor reflection as in a mirror; then we shall see face to face. Now I know in part; then I shall know fully, even as I am fully known" (1 Corinthians 13:12).

Humble and Holy Father,
The more I learn about myself, the more I realize my
need for You. And the more I get to know You, the more
amazed I am that You delight in knowing me. Open my
eyes to see beyond what's in front of me that I might live
more fully for You. Open my ears to hear what You're
saying above the clamor and strivings of this world.
Settle my heart to know that it's through intimacy and
abiding that my life will bear much fruit. Enlarge my
heart to love others no matter what the world thinks of
them. Take me by the hand and lead me along the un-
common path that I might know and give the other-
worldly love You have given me. Precious Savior, lead
me on. Amen.

Declaration:
I declare by faith that I am an anointed, righteous,
woman of God! Jesus has forgiven me; He has redeemed me; and He has restored me! I refuse to buy
into the world's value system of façade and appear-
ances. I will treasure and value what is true and
lovely and worthy of praise. I embrace the truth that
I am seated with Christ, and that never changes! I
refuse insecurity, anxiety, and petty jealousies. I am
determined to see others with eyes of faith and hope
and love. I will be quick to listen and to pray, and
slow to assume and to judge. I am more committed
to the truth than to making people think well of me.
And I will walk in the Lord's presence as I live here
on earth (Psalm 116:9)!

what about you?

1. We as women, at one time or another, have all done what I call "shadowboxing." In other words, we perceive what we think someone else may be thinking, and in our anger we react to that perception. In our minds we get mad, react, and then defend ourselves. And then, based on little or no factual information, we soon find ourselves swinging at the air because of a perceived conflict with an opponent who is totally unaware of their offense or our feelings. Think about a time when this happened to you or someone you know. Describe a better and uncommon response to such a situation.

2. Proverbs 9:10 tells us that knowing the Holy One results in understanding. The more we know God's heart, the more we appreciate the work of His hands. The more we trust His intentions, the more we entrust ourselves to Him. Look back over this past year of walking with God. Do you see anything differently today than you did a year ago? Have certain values or convictions changed? Explain.

3. Read 1 John 3:1. Read it again, slowly. This is a profound verse. Divide this verse into three parts (I'm looking at the *New International Version*).

   • When was the last time you just marinated in the presence of God? In other words, how often do you slow down long enough to "catch" all of the love He is pouring out for you? Write down a prayer declaring that you receive all of the love He so willingly longs to give.

- Being identified as someone the Creator loves totally affects our identity. How has being associated with Jesus affected your identity? How has it affected your everyday life? Explain.

- In what ways do you feel misunderstood by the world because of your belief system? How does that make you feel? Explain.

4. Read 1 John 3:2, and again, read it slowly. This verse makes my knees weak. Describe in your own words what you think this verse means. Ask the Holy Spirit to give you a fresh revelation and insight into this passage.

5. Read 1 John 3:3. Though we spend millions of dollars trying to improve ourselves, and way too much energy trying to prove ourselves, what we really need is to be purified. The pure in heart see God. Dare to take a look inside at your areas of striving and angst, and bring those things to the light before God. Set your hope on Him. Write down a prayer committing these areas to the Lord. Ask Him to renew your heart and your perspective.

*We who earned banishment
shall enjoy communion; we who deserve
the pains of hell shall know the bliss
of heaven.*[1]

≫ A. W. TOZER

Speak and act as those who are going to be judged
by the law that gives freedom, because
judgment without mercy will be shown to
anyone who has not been merciful.
Mercy triumphs over judgment.

≫ JAMES 2:12–13

chooses mercy over judgment

The phone cord wrapped around my toes as I sat sideways in my chair; I listened intently to what my friend had to say, and I didn't want to miss a thing.

"Susie, I don't know what's going on lately. I know you are really hurting right now because of what these women have been saying about you, but I have to admit I too have been tempted to turn on you, for no particular reason. It's like the enemy is working overtime, tempting those who have it in them to cross the line from friendship to betrayal. When 'so-and-so' talked to me about you, for the briefest moment I wanted to jump in and add fuel to the fire. But then I remembered God, and I remembered you.

"I turned the conversation around and challenged this woman to think about what she was saying. I know you are someone who wants nothing more than to walk closely with the Lord. I appreciate how open you are to receive correction. But it's almost like you've given the world a freeway to your inner soul on which to drive up and say anything, anytime, and then it's somehow okay to make you responsible for everything.

"It's like you subconsciously give off a message that makes other women subconsciously think, 'I could be ugly to this person and get away with it.' Even generally mature Christian women have it in them to be petty to other women, and when they are faced with the temptation to be rude and wrong, only the fear of God will make them walk away from such a situation.

"I know this painful season has wounded you, but as long as you think it's okay for everyone and anyone to confront you, you will be a target for this kind of battle. I'm not saying you shouldn't be teachable, because I know you always will be. I'm not saying that you are responsible for what other women are doing to you because they will have to give an account for their actions.

"I am just saying you might want to close down that freeway by building a stronger boundary around your walk of faith. You walk closely with the Lord. The Holy Spirit will convict you when you need it. You've got godly, trusted friends. They will lovingly correct you when you need it. Don't give women (especially ones who have no fear of God) any more permission to devastate you this way.

"It was only my own fear of God that kept me from being one of those women who hurt you deeply. Once the temptation lifted, I was overwhelmed with gratitude that our friendship was still intact, along with my conscience."

꩜

My friend's words changed me. I did build a healthy boundary around my heart, and I am a different person because of it. I've stayed teachable, but I now hang on to who I am while learning life's lessons. When we are wounded or attacked, we must remember Christ's example of humility. But in our remembering we do not lose sight of who we are and whose we are.

In the book of Isaiah chapter 50, in one breath the prophet says, "I offered my back to those who beat me . . .", and yet in another he declares, "Because the Sovereign Lord helps me, I will not be disgraced. . . . I set my face like flint, and I know I will not be ashamed. He who vindicates me is near" (vv. 6–8). Humble response. Confident belief. To be strong in the Lord is to be confident in Him. To be teachable under His care is to allow Him to use whatever means necessary to make us more like Him.

To be transformable is to give the Lord (along with trusted godly people) easy access to the things of our character that Jesus might make us more like Him. But opening our souls up to anyone who wants to say a cross word to us is not wise. Not to say we should keep difficult people out of our lives. *They* are usually the ones God uses to refine our character. But we must not give more weight to their words than those of our godly friends and wonderful Savior.

Giving people easy access to dethrone our identity and devastate us is not healthy. Deep in our souls there must be an inner chamber where only Jesus resides. It's in that place where Jesus sits on the throne of our lives. By His very presence there, we are made, and continually being made whole. He has already decided our worth, so it must never be up for grabs again. Since we belong to God, we can *rule* in the midst of our enemies (see Psalm 110:2).

Some people are just plain mean; and others, misguided. We can be kind to these people, but we don't have to let them (or their words) in. Others might be on to something when they point out our flaws, but if they possess no fear of God, we must confidently leave their presence and bring ourselves before the Lord. In that *safe* and holy place we confess our sin, admit our need for Him, and then throw ourselves on the *mercy* of heaven's court.

A friend of mine had a mentor who had a great saying whenever mixed messages or attitudes were thrown at her that were in disagreement with God's voice and His Word. When careless words or names were tossed her way, she simply responded by saying to herself, *I won't wear that.*

As I mentioned in an earlier chapter, in order for us to thrive in these latter days, there *must* be a bigger gap between how people affect us, and how God affects us. We cannot grow in our capacity to love others if we never settle the issue that we are loved. Sometimes we think we must let go of one to take hold of the other, but this makes no sense.

We hold close our identity. We allow God's love and mercy to transform us. We humbly give mercy away. And when bullies or misguided people treat us terribly, we forgive them and refuse to become hardened by the encounter. With all our hearts we believe that in the end, our Living and Holy God will settle every issue and every account.

Sometimes the act of being a doormat is mistaken for true humility, and yet these two are polar opposites. True humility *never* lets go of identity. Our identification with Christ is the bedrock of who we are and must *never* be a moveable option in our lives. Out of our Christ-connection springs our attitudes and choices.

The "fruit" of doormat theology is never life-giving. When we put ourselves under the feet of others in some warped belief that having their footprints on our back is a martyrlike thing to do, we make light of true martyrdom. Moreover, after we've allowed someone to walk all over us, we tend to feel mad, resentful, depressed, oppressed, or simply worth *less*. None of these things come from the Vine.

If we only *partially* believe that God's divine love and forgiveness are true for us, we will walk with a spiritual limp and thus be an easy target for attack; easy to take advantage of. If we *truly* accept Christ's mercy, we will walk along in holy confidence. We will rely on His mercy, and we'll freely give it as we've received it.

When mercy flows in us, mercy flows through us. Functioning from that place allows us to serve and give out of fullness, not emptiness. And when we encounter difficulties along the way, we face them with all of the holy confidence in the world. What kind of fruit comes from *true* humility? Love, joy, peace, patience, kindness, gentleness . . .

True humility allows us to bow before Jesus when we are under fire because we know He is in the fire with us. Our battleground becomes a sacred place because though we are at that moment in great need, we've not let go of who we are to God and who He is to us. Can you see the difference here? Doormat theology focuses on us, and true humility keeps us seated on the throne with *Him*.

☙

I shared the opening story for two reasons. For one, I cherished my friend's honesty and I truly valued her insight. She is a godly, trusted friend, and she had every right to speak into my life. She serves as an excellent example for us all. And she makes a good point. We avoid judging others not by trying hard, but because we love and fear God more than we like and enjoy playing with someone else's dirt. We walk under His protection when we value what He says. This is what He says:

"Do not judge others, and you will not be judged. For you will be treated as you treat others. The standard you use in judging, is the standard by which you will be judged" (Matthew 7:1–2 NLT).

Look at the second sentence in that verse: *For you will be treated as you treat others*. Think about it. We have the obvious interpretation that if we treat others with contempt, we will be treated as such. A very basic truth, no? One we should keep with us wherever we go. This verse harmonizes with the Bible's sowing and reaping principles.

But I want us to scoot in a little closer and look at a profound truth hidden in this verse: *If you treat others like they have power over you and your identity, they will treat you as though they have power over you and your identity.*

Conversely, when you walk in the truth of who you are, you are telling others the truth about who they are. Loved. Called. Chosen. Forgiven.

When you believe a lie, you are in turn lying to others.

"Do not lie to each other, since you have taken off your old self with its practices and have put on the new self, which is being renewed in knowledge in the image of its Creator" (Colossians 3:9–10).

Whether others like us or not, forgive us or not, give us the benefit of the doubt or not, we get to stand with Christ. Mercy allows us to be linked in fellowship with Him. Humility never lets go of identity.

My second reason for sharing this story begs us to dig a little deeper. Have you ever noticed how we have all walked through seasons when the "grace has lifted"? Not God's grace for us. Never that. But how about the grace others *normally* have for us? I've seen it over and over again. It makes me wonder if the enemy sometimes approaches God like he did with Job and asks, "Let me sift her, just a little bit. I just want to sharpen the air around her and make her *seem* less appealing. Maybe then you will see her true colors and those of her so-called friends."

God allowed Job to be sifted and Job came forth as gold. God never tempts us, but He allows us to be tempted. Tests are an indicator of how far we've come. Trials prove us. Because God is intent on making the most of every opportunity, He allows each trial to spill over and touch anyone who will learn from it.

I wasn't the only one being tested and proven during my "grace-less" hour. A handful of the women in my life were also being tested when they were tempted to jump on the bandwagon. This is not to say that I was completely innocent of transgression and only going through the fire because God loves me so much.

I had irritating flaws then and I have irritating flaws now. Just like you. But I wasn't willfully sinning during this time. In fact, I had godly friends who were scratching their heads, wondering what in the world was going on. One friend even said, "It's like God is allowing you to experience an out-of-proportion level of accountability so you can feel how He feels about how we women treat each other."

Whatever the reason that trial took place those many years ago, I spent a portion of it curled up in a ball, covering my head from the flaming arrows, and wondering if and how I would ever survive such a thing.

When we come upon another woman's grace-less hour and we are tempted to find fault and nitpick, we must remember mercy. We must remember grace. We must not forget the basin.

You'll easily find kindling in her character; things easy to point out; perfect for the fire. You'll find kernels of truth in what you hear and what you see. Even so, don't fall for the enemy's trap in thinking you're the one who has it together and she is one who is the putz. Seasons come and seasons go. The grace lifts from us and it rests upon us again.

Apart from Christ, none of us "has it together." What we do during someone else's grace-less hour will have a direct impact on us when our time of testing comes. We will either be strengthened in the Lord, or be disciplined by Him.

Walk carefully when you come upon another woman who seems to be the hot topic of conversation. She—and those in her circle of influence—may be enduring a time of testing to see what is in them.

Be uncommon. Stop the flow of words. Increase the awareness of God's presence in the situation by acknowledging His love, His forgiveness, and His mercy to those who are open to it. Refuse to be a nonthinking-all-too-common woman who simply jumps on the bandwagon because that's where the party is. Walk away from women who love to fuel the fire. Pray for them, but walk away.

Step back and imagine yourself in the middle of the fire. What response would mean the world to you? Humility? Understanding? Giving the benefit of the doubt? Be that person. Do those things.

Never (no, never) forget that you stand and live and breathe because of undeserved forgiveness. When faced with the opportunity to spew judgment or extend mercy, extend mercy.

                         ⁓ॐ⁓

She rolled over in bed and blinked her eyes shut, hoping to chase away the emptiness that threatened to consume her. She pulled her knees to her chest and clutched her blanket. Her thoughts drifted back to when she was a little girl. Her favorite pastime was to run and skip through the woods that led to the creek.

She loved flicking her feet through the water causing sprays of droplets to bounce off the top of the pond. The warmth of the sun, the sounds of the birds, and the freedom of her private sanctuary somehow gave her the sense that she was protected.

Pain exploded through her shoulder as they jerked her out of bed. Her mind shot from her past to the immediate present in a matter of seconds. The men were much larger than she and did not need to squeeze her arm so tightly . . . but they did.

"Adulterer!" they shouted as they dragged her from her bedroom, leaving the other adulterer alone to roll over and sleep off his hangover. To resist their brute strength would be foolish, but to be humiliated in front of the townspeople would be devastating.

Little pebbles and sharp stones scraped her feet as they dragged her faster than she could walk. When they finally started to slow down enough for her to catch her footing, they threw her to the ground. Pain grinded in her chin as it smashed into the gravel.

"This is the end for me," she thought. Her throat thickened as the crowd pressed in. She swallowed slowly when she heard sounds of the mob picking up sticks and stones.[2]

⁓◎⁓

As [Jesus] was speaking, the teachers of religious law and the Pharisees brought a woman who had been caught in the act of adultery. They put her in front of the crowd. "Teacher," they said to Jesus, "this woman was caught in the act of adultery. The law of Moses says to stone her. What do you say?" They kept demanding an answer, so he stood up again and said, "All right, but let the one who has never sinned throw the first stone!" Then he stooped down again and wrote in the dust. When the accusers heard this, they slipped away one by one, beginning with the oldest, until only Jesus was left in the middle of the crowd with the woman. (John 8:3–5, 7–10 NLT)

The woman was in bed with a man who wasn't her husband. She was embroiled in scandal. She was guilty. We have names for women who do such things. And yet, how does our Savior handle such a person?

He stooped down. He knelt on the gravel. He wrote in the dust. He got His hands dirty while keeping His heart pure. Isn't that just amazing? What a radical and powerful example Jesus modeled for us.

The Pharisees *put her in front of the crowd.* Just think about that for a moment. We do the same thing when we choose judgment over mercy. I find it interesting that the stones fell out of the hands of the oldest people first. Could it be that they had lived long enough to know how guilty they were? Do the young still tend to possess an inflated sense of self-righteousness? Maybe so. Maybe that's why gossip is rampant among younger women. But they are not the only ones.

Either way, it's time for a change. With all my heart I believe God's patience is running out for women who call themselves Christians and yet think nothing of participating in slicing-and-dicing conversations that leave their sisters bleeding on the roadside.

When I speak at retreats and I give the Basin message, women come forward in droves, usually weeping, almost always broken. They are either reeling from the pain of someone else's gossip, or they are deeply convicted for the pain they've inflicted. What's beautiful, though, is that *they come forward—to Jesus—and they receive His mercy and His kindness*, and He puts them on their feet again.

Though we may find plenty of stones at our feet, we have no right to use them. Even if we are accurate in our perception of another hard-to-love woman, we still don't get to throw rocks at her. Look what happened to the adulterous woman when the sinners all backed away from her—she was standing alone with Jesus. Can you think of a better place for the outright sinner *or* the unjustly judged? The most wonderful thing we can do for the woman under attack is to bring her before Jesus.

"My dear friends, don't let public opinion influence how you live out our glorious, Christ-originated faith" (James 2:1 THE MESSAGE).

❧

When we remember that Jesus washed the feet of *every* disciple, not just the eleven, but Judas too, we remember the kind of heart He has. When we betray and say things and do things that are beneath us, we are once again so thankful for God's heart and fresh mercies.

Daily mercy is offered to us. And daily it needs to be offered through us. Modern-day Pharisees don't like mercy. They much prefer judgment. Religious people take it upon themselves to police and judge the sins of the people. They exact harsh verdicts against others and demand that people live by a standard they themselves could never abide by. This is a miserable way to live.

Just after Jesus washed the disciples' feet, He told His followers that no servant is greater than his master. He encouraged them to follow *His example*. We must not think for a minute that our judgments trump God's mercy. On the contrary, our own judgments condemn us. In other words, when we judge, we take ourselves out from under the umbrella of God's grace and choose instead to live by the letter of the law, which condemns. We stay on the low road to build our case. We seek the high road to gain perspective.

Every time we judge, or build a case, or just plain gossip, we are acting out of a lie. When we *react* to someone's actions rather than *respond* to God's love, we act out of a lie. When we believe that another person has the power to diminish our worth, we are staring a lie in the face. When someone is so ugly that we can't help but return the favor—we are acting human, but we are still believing a lie. We all get out of step at times. And that's okay, as long as we find our way back to the uncommon path once again.

Stay close to Him and become a source of refreshment for many. Love and mercy change a heart when judgment never could.

So get rid of all evil behavior. Be done with deceit, hypocrisy, jealousy, and all unkind speech. . . . Be careful to live properly among your unbelieving neighbors. Then even if they accuse you of doing wrong, they will see your honorable behavior, and they will give honor to God when he judges the world. . . . It is God's will that your honorable lives should silence those ignorant people who make foolish accusations against you. For you are free, yet you are God's slaves, so don't use your freedom as an excuse to do evil. Respect everyone, and love your Christian brothers and sisters. Fear God.

(1 Peter 2:1, 12, 15–17 NLT)

> *Wherever and whenever God appears to men, He acts like Himself. Whether in the Garden of Eden or the Garden of Gethsemane, God is merciful as well as just. He has always dealt in mercy with mankind and will always deal in justice when His mercy is despised.*[3]
>
> A. W. TOZER

Precious Jesus,
You are all that I need. Forgive me, Lord, for the times
I've held on to judgment and forsaken mercy. Every
day, You offer mercy to me. Every day. This perpetual
gift is a priceless one, and I don't want to miss a drop of
your morning mercies. Bring to mind those who need
mercy from me. Show me any hidden judgments that
I've neglected to bring into the light. Refresh me in
Your presence and draw near as I pray. Help me to love
mercy, Lord, the way You love me. What a treasure it
is to belong to You. Lead me on, for Your name's sake.
Amen.

Declaration:
In Jesus' Name I declare that I am an uncommon woman! I walk under the daily mercies of God, and I enjoy a heart at peace. When other women rise up

against me, I bow low and entrust myself to my
Savior. You are my defense, and I will not be
moved. I am holy and confident, a humbly dependent woman of God. I know who I am and I know
where I'm going. I am a faithful friend, full of integrity, and abounding in love. I refuse the bandwagon, and I choose the high road. I walk in the
Lord's presence as I live here on earth. Hallelujah!

what about you?

1. Read James 2:12–13. When we judge, we "try, give a
   ruling on, conclude, surmise, conjecture, regard as,
   rate as, reckon, appraise, examine."[4]

   Read over this list slowly and search your own
   heart. Write down the initials of people whom you
   are currently judging according to the above de-
   scription. Spend some time praying over this list.
   Ask the Lord for forgiveness. Pray for your offend-
   ers. Be refreshed in God's presence.

2. When we show mercy, we show "clemency, compassion, grace, charity, forgiveness, soft-heartedness,
   tender-heartedness, kindness, generosity, magna-
   nimity."[5]

   Read over this list slowly. Think of the instances
   in the Bible where mercy was shown. Moses put
   himself between the people and God and assumed
   their need. God wanted to destroy them for how
   they treated Moses. Jesus went before the Father on

our behalf. This is a foreign way to respond to an offense. Pick two aspects of mercy and write your thoughts about them. Describe a time when you showed mercy. What was that like for you? Explain.

3. Read 1 John 2:9. Rewrite this verse in your own words and apply it to women. Explain how bad attitudes can darken your perspective on life.

4. Read 1 John 2:10. What a powerful thought! Why do you suppose Scripture suggests that when we truly love others we are protected from stumbling? Explain.

5. Read Proverbs 26:20 and write down a few tangible ways you can apply this verse.

Walking with God down the avenues of prayer we acquire something of His likeness, and unconsciously we become witnesses to others of His beauty and His grace.[1]

&E. M. BOUNDS

Make this your common practice: Confess your sins to each other and pray for each other so that you can live together whole and healed. The prayer of a person living right with God is something powerful to be reckoned with.

&JAMES 5:16 THE MESSAGE

chooses prayer
over pettiness

Joab walked directly in front of David, looked down on him, and began roaring his frustrations. "Many times he almost speared you to death in his castle. I've seen that with my own eyes. Furthermore, the whole world believes the lies he tells about you. He has come, the King himself, hunting every cave, pit and hole on earth to find you and kill you like a dog. But tonight you had him at the end of his own spear and you did nothing!"

This time it was David's answer that blazed with fire. "Better he kill me than I become as he is. I shall not practice the ways that cause kings to go mad. I will not throw spears, nor will I allow hatred to grow in my heart. I will not avenge. Not now. Not ever!"

Angels went to bed that night . . . and dreamed, in the afterglow of that rare, rare day, that God might yet be able to give His authority to a trustworthy vessel.[2]

This passage was taken from Gene Edward's powerful book *The Tale of Three Kings: A Study in Brokenness*. Please read this book if you ever get the chance.

David was anointed and appointed to be king one day. Saul

wore the crown but it didn't fit him. He had the palace and the position but no heart. Saul allowed his wicked insecurities to drive him mad. His raging jealousy toward David translated into many attempts on David's life. Rather than learning to humbly walk with God, Saul repeatedly took matters into his own dirty hands and became increasingly earthbound as a result.

David ran for his life. And during those moments when his lungs begged for air and his heart pounded in his chest, he trusted the One who gave him his humble, kinglike heart. David crouched down behind rocks and in crevices on the mountainside, and yet his belief in the faithfulness of God spanned farther than the horizon. Though he struggled with perspective at times, his faith in God almost always surpassed his natural circumstances.

David was the most amazing warrior of his time, but because He walked closely with God, he understood that this was not the time to fight. David hid instead. He hid in the shelter of God's wings. He prayed. He prayed for God to vindicate him. And he worshiped. This cave dweller turned his humble hideout into a holy sanctuary. When David worshiped, he knew God was there with him. Because God inhabits the praises of His people, David wrapped himself in a garment of praise. David knelt his scraped knees on the rocky cave floor, and he lifted his calloused hands in praise to the One his eyes could not see. And when he did, the power of the Living God strengthened him for the road ahead. David humbled himself under the mighty hand of God, knowing that one day he would be free to fulfill his destiny.

☙ ❧

During Passover week, Jesus rode into Jerusalem on a donkey. All eyes were on Him as the crowds adoringly waved their palm branches through the air. Jesus humbly rode through the sea of people amidst the noise and the songs and the cheers. So large was the crowd that the Jewish leaders actually lamented, "We've lost. Look, the whole world has gone after Him!" (Read John 12:17–19.)

News of healings, deliverances, and other kinds of miracles spread from town to town. I imagine women whispering about Him at the well, men debating about Him on the roadside, and children listening in while watching the clouds change shape before their eyes. The air must have felt different when God became man.

Folks came from all around to get a firsthand look at the radical One everybody was talking about. The people were swept up in the excitement of it all. They were there for the show, and not so much for their Savior. In only a matter of hours, they would be engrossed in a different kind of fervor—the execution of an innocent man. The very One they had previously treated like a king.

People are fickle. Groupthink is a powerful force. When we listen to others spew their condemning opinions about others, our own thoughts begin to run wild. And when our thoughts are no longer held at bay by our holy conviction, words start to flow. And when words start to flow, so goes the current of petty behaviors and wrong perspectives. If we're not careful, we will get swept up in a movement that *seems* right, but in the end leads to death (see Proverbs 16:25).

"If the godly give in to the wicked, it's like polluting a fountain or muddying a spring" (Proverbs 25:26 NLT).

If, when faced with the flaws in others, we compromise with the wicked, we muddy the waters of our witness. But we don't just muddy the waters. It's worse than that. We wound someone who was shaped and formed in God's image.

Never mind if God's imprint is difficult to see, it's still there. When we wound someone He has made, we wound Him. And every time we give way to the urge to be rude or petty, we pave a Saul-like path in our lives. Before we know it, our *instinctive* response will be to go down that road and our choices will begin to reflect the lack of character within.

But if, when facing another's foibles, we dialogue with God instead, we will change the spiritual climate around us. Like David, we must sincerely pray, confidently live, and humbly respond when others have it out for us. And when we do this, we turn our rocky paths and our dark caves into holy ground. When*ever* we come up against the fallen nature of another, we have a divine opportunity to bring a little of heaven to earth. But this is rarely the easy way.

Walking away from low conversations is an uncommon thing to do. Choosing to pray when it's easier to be petty is an uncommon thing to do. Yet to humbly bow our knee and dialogue with God is to *feast* at His table. Rather than being weakened by *talking about* someone's rudeness, we are strengthened by *talking to* the One who is good. Instead of feeling self-righteous because of the momentary distraction of someone else's sin, we feel gratefully aware of His mercy because we are painfully aware that we need it.

Spending time in His presence gives us insight into His perspective and reminds us again of His love . . . for *everyone*. When we begin seeing things as He sees them, we begin saying what He would say.

The Bible says that we will eat the words of our mouth (see Proverbs 18:21). If we are talking trash, we are eating trash. When a person eats trash, their life gives off a noxious gas and their breath just smells bad. On the other hand, when we *taste* and see that the Lord is good, and when our words agree with His Word, we give off the fragrance of the Living God. We bear the fruit that comes from being connected to the Vine.

We—as uncommon and beloved women of the Most High God—are to be a source of refreshment to others. When we walk closely with the Lord, we become a flow-through account of blessing and encouragement.

When we step away from our divine call to be uncommon, we muddy the waters. Instead of enjoying a cool drink when others encounter us, they swallow the sand and the dirt in our speech. Instead of nourishing them, we weaken them.

Every time another woman bothers us, we are faced with a choice. Every time. We can either pray for the things we see in her (and ask that *we* would have more grace for others), or we can carry a grudge with us so the next time her name comes up, we have something to throw in the pile.

Many of the things we bump up against in other women would be settled if we would do these three things:

❖ *Give them the benefit of the doubt.*

❖ *Pray for them.*

❖ *Entrust them to God.*

But that's not usually our first response. We tend to be highly offendable creatures and have a hard time letting go of things. Instead of walking away from the wad of gum on the hot asphalt, we pick it up. It sticks to our fingers and then gets on our clothes. Then we need help from others to get all the goop off us. Before we know it, we have a whole community involved in our sticky situation when it would have been better just to walk away and let it be.

How many times have you spoken too soon and, in doing so, unleashed a whirlwind of conversation and drama that never needed to happen? Do you know what the by-product of misspoken words is? It's anxiety. Stirring up trouble with your words will bring a dust storm of stress and anxiety to your door.

Most of the time people get to us when *we're* not right. People are made in the image of Christ, and when we walk closely with Christ and allow *His peace* to rule in our hearts, loving others is truly a joy.

Not to say that we won't have legitimate reasons for irritation, frustration, or just plain anger. We will. Jesus promised us as much. But still, He tells us to be of good cheer, to let peace rule in us, and to love mercy. When we are in step with our Savior, it's easier for us to love those who are out of step or on a different path altogether.

One of my pastor's mentors once spoke these wise words: "God will bless you or afflict you with people according to your need."[3] God is never surprised when we come upon a difficult person, though I'm quite sure some of our reactions give Him pause.

It doesn't matter if the other person is deserving of our verbal spewing; it's always about what kind of response God deserves from us. And what He deserves from us is a sincere and loving relationship. Continual dialogue. Kingdom passion. Calvary love. Words that build up and bless. Prayers that move mountains *and* molehills.

Besides, it's confusing for new believers and pre-believers when we gossip. We give them mixed messages when just after we mudsling someone with our words, we head off to worship practice, Bible study, or to sew a quilt for the local children's hospital.

"With the tongue we praise our Lord and Father, and with it we curse women, who have been made in God's likeness. Out of the same mouth come praise and cursing. My sisters, this should not be" (see James 3:9–10).

When a miserable, angry person gossips, it's easy to consider the source. But when an otherwise "good" or godly person gossips, their words are especially lethal. Though her tongue has yet to be conquered, she possesses other areas of strength and virtue, which give her a measure of credibility. That's why the "godly gossip" does so much damage in the body of Christ.

Furthermore, the areas in which we judge others are the very areas in which we are susceptible to temptation or even failure.

People mirror us. Most times we are irritated with others because they are reflecting back an amplification of something we greatly dislike about ourselves.

I remember a time when I felt frustrated with a woman who continually got herself into trouble by overcommitting her time. Months later I went through a major burnout because I had been repeatedly overcommitting my time. We often see ourselves in others, and we don't like it very much. They need mercy. We need mercy. Mercy always triumphs over judgment. Prayer always swallows up pettiness. Always.

Our tongue is like a sharp blade. When a surgeon holds a blade, she aims to heal. Her blade separates that which brings death from that which offers life. When an intruder holds a blade, she aims to offend, to wound, or to possibly kill.

We were born and appointed for this day in which we live. With the trouble and pain and dysfunction all around us, we have within our words the capacity to heal, encourage, reconcile, and restore. We, by the power of the Holy Spirit, through our prayers and our words, can help others discern that which brings life from that which diminishes it.

But we also have the capacity to do great harm. Either way, we will *eat* the fruit of what comes out of our mouth.

> The tongue has the power of life and death, and those who love it will eat its fruit. (Proverbs 18:21)
>
> A gentle answer turns away wrath, but a harsh word stirs up anger. (Proverbs 15:1)
>
> The tongue that brings healing is a tree of life but a deceitful tongue crushes the spirit. (Proverbs 15:4)
>
> An unreliable messenger stumbles into trouble, but a reliable messenger brings healing. (Proverbs 13:17 NLT)

That last verse especially touched me. No matter how we look at it, we are messengers. May God's message of reconciliation not get lost in translation by the way we live and by the way we speak. May we be women who are much with God. May we be a generation of women who are powerful in prayer.

⟃⟄

Guard your heart above all else, for it determines the course of your life. (Proverbs 4:23 NLT)

Whole books have been written on the power of the tongue. Words have started wars, dissolved marriages, and ended friendships. But is it enough to curb our words? If we zip our lips while our hearts are raging, we are only halfway there.

Yes, we must exercise self-restraint with our words, and every time we do, we will be profoundly glad we did. But as uncommon women the call is much higher. We need to talk often with the Lord. We need to listen to Him. We must allow Him to search our hearts and point out anything that might offend Him (see Psalm 139). We need to go to the deepest places of our hearts and allow God's kindness to bring us to repentance.

When we face our own capacity for ugliness and pettiness, and then we look to Jesus and find only mercy, we are humbled. We are grateful. When we ask the Lord's forgiveness for our sinful attitudes, we actually come away refreshed.

We find a vital dose of courage and strength when we humble ourselves and *accept* God's mercy. We are *lifted up* when we bow down. When we kneel before our Maker and brokenly confess our need, God considers *that moment* and *that place* a high and holy place to be. Consider and imagine what God is saying here; it's profound.

The high and lofty one who lives in eternity, the Holy One, says this: "I live in the high and holy place with those whose spirits are contrite and humble. I restore the crushed spirit of the humble and revive the courage of those with repentant hearts. (Isaiah 57:15 NLT)

When we really trust that God is a God of justice and He will eventually confront our bullies, we can say along with King David, "May the Lord judge between us. Perhaps the Lord will punish you for what you are trying to do to me, but I will never harm you" (1 Samuel 24:12 NLT).

When others bewilder us with their behavior, we must remember that *we too* have a past. If I am being real, I have to admit that I have behaved in ways that make me cringe; sinned in ways that have debunked my witness; and loved in ways that make people wonder how I treat my enemies.

We *all* have places in our own story we would rather forget. And if we allow him to, the enemy will earmark those pages in our book so we are reminded of them again and again. Even while you read, Jesus is writing a new chapter in your life. Again today He tells us to forget the past—and not to dwell on it—because He is doing a new thing! We don't have to revisit those pages in our story unless our healing process requires that we do so.

Always, when the call is present for us to be nobler and take the higher way, we must remember that Jesus doesn't ask anything *of* us that He hasn't already done *for* us. In order for us to choose prayer over pettiness, we need to revel in the fact that Jesus constantly intercedes for us. When we thoroughly embrace the fact that we've been thoroughly embraced, we are more able to love the unlovely.

When you feel out of sorts and critical of everyone around you, that's the perfect time to find a quiet place, look up in the sky, and allow yourself to enjoy the love of the Lord. Talk to Him. Let Him talk to you. Use that time to clear out some of your muddled thoughts and replace them with the idea that Jesus is singing over you. He is pulling for you. He wants you to receive from Him what He so lovingly wants to give more of Himself.

Over and over again the Bible tells us to *remember what God has done*. When we remember what God has done, we will be more apt to do what He would do.

A. W. Tozer penned a wonderful perspective on God's absolute forgiveness and acceptance of us. While you read, allow yourself to be overwhelmed with gratitude that we have a God in whom there is no pettiness, no drama, no gossip, and no manipulation. Only pure, unadulterated love. Absolutely amazing.

> How unutterably sweet is the knowledge that our Heavenly Father knows us completely. No talebearer can inform on us, no enemy can make an accusation stick; no forgotten skeleton can come tumbling out of some hidden closet to abash us and expose our past; no unsuspected weakness in our characters can come to light to turn God away from us, since He knew us utterly before we knew Him and called us to Himself in the full knowledge of everything that was against us.[4]

On the night He was betrayed, Jesus took the bread and broke it. He thanked God as He said to His disciples, "This is my body, given for you; do this in remembrance of me." On that same night, Jesus lifted up the cup of wine, thanked His Father, and said, "This is my blood, poured out for you, for the forgiveness of sins; a token of the new and everlasting covenant. Do this in remembrance of me." (Read Luke 22:17–20.)

Though His betrayal was *in motion*, He served Communion. He reclined at the table in the presence of His enemy. Jesus knew that in a few short hours He would face rejection, torture, and execution. And with the longing and passion of His humble heart, He looked forward to getting His disciples around the table for the sake of communion.

Before His followers had a chance to be traumatized by the devil's evil schemes, Jesus put a flag in the ground. In so many words, He said to them, "*Remember this. Remember us.* Remember that the enemy hasn't taken my life; I have freely given it. Remember that though your badness once disqualified you, the Father's goodness has saved you. *This* is the new covenant. Remember that though I am well aware of what lies ahead of me on that cross, My deepest desire beforehand is to be with you, break bread with you, and remind you that My promises are true. Though schemes are being devised behind My back, I want you, My beloved ones, to see My face."

Oh, the love of Jesus.

How many times do you suppose that night was replayed in the minds of the disciples? Did the impact of Jesus' actions have an increasingly greater place in their lives as they grew in their faith over the years? And what does this scene have to do with prayer versus pettiness?

I just can't get this phrase out of my mind: "*On the night He was betrayed*, He took the bread and broke it, saying this is My body, given up for *you*." As if that night was one seamless Kingly piece of fabric, Jesus served, loved, and amidst the plan against His life, reminded us to remember Him.

Outside, the soldiers were receiving their orders to find and capture a rebel. Inside, the King of the universe was preparing to go to the Cross. Empty accusations. Kingdom response.

If we're more bent toward pettiness than we are toward prayer, we need to step away from our imagined rights (the way Jesus stepped away from the table) and simply remember *Him*. When we take Communion, we must seriously consider what lives in our hearts and what fuels our motivations. As we grasp more and more the unexplainable wonder of His love, we'll want to talk with Him first about everything that troubles us. And when we talk with Him, *He* refreshes us.

As uncommon women, our call is a high one.

Every time an angry or irritable thought comes to mind, turn your back on it and pray instead. This is not denial; this is your spiritual strategy. This is your chance to foil one of the devil's schemes. This is your opportunity to carry on the work of the Kingdom.

Every time you are in a crowd of gossips, if you don't have the courage to confront the current, walk away and pray instead. Guard your heart and mind with all diligence. Consider your fellowship with God much more important than your popularity with the crowd.

Every time you are tempted to throw fuel on the fire, stop yourself and ask your friends, "Can we just pray right now? I don't want this conversation to keep going this way." And if your friends don't wrap their arms around you and passionately say, "Oh, yes! You are so right! Thank you for having the courage and conviction to say that!" then you might want to find some new friends.

Ask God to make you a holy, honorable woman. Ask Him to move in the lives of your friends. Ask Him to give you eyes to see the hard-to-love the way He does. Ask Him to make you more passionate in prayer and earnest for His presence. Know that He diligently rewards those who run after Him.

Shake off the dust of pettiness and pursue the higher road of prayer. Treasures await you there, and you will be transformed along the way. And remember, never trust anyone with things that shouldn't be said.

Love must be sincere. Hate what is evil; cling to what is good. Be devoted to one another in [sisterly] love. Honor one another above yourselves. Never be lacking in zeal, but keep your spiritual fervor, serving the Lord. Be joyful in hope, patient in affliction, faithful in prayer. Share with God's people who are in need. Practice hospitality. Bless those who persecute you; bless and do not curse. Rejoice with those who rejoice; mourn with those who mourn. Live in harmony with one another. Do not be proud, but be willing to associate with people of low position. Do not be conceited. Do not repay anyone evil for evil. Be careful to do what is right in the eyes of everybody. If it is possible, as far as it depends on you, live at peace with everyone. Do not take revenge, my friends, but leave room for God's wrath, for it is written: "It is mine to avenge; I will repay," says the Lord. On the contrary: "If your enemy is hungry, feed him; if he is thirsty, give him something to drink. In doing this, you will heap burning coals on his head." Do not be overcome by evil, but overcome evil with good. (Romans 12:9–21)

> *Our prayer life will become restful when it really dawns upon us that we have done all we are supposed to do when we have spoken to Him about it. From that moment we have left it with Him. It is His responsibility.*[5]
>
> O. HALLESBY

Precious Lord,
I ask Your forgiveness for every time I've chosen petti-
ness over prayer. Forgive me for so easily giving in to
catty thoughts and useless words. I long to be an uncom-
mon woman. I am an uncommon woman! Fill me up
afresh with a sense of Your love and holiness. Compel
me to walk in a more noble way. Draw me to prayer.
Speak to me when I'm there. And help me to listen.

I want to change the world by the way that I live.
Thank You for leaving me with such a tangible exam-
ple of what true and humble love looks like. Continue
Your good work in me. In Your name, I pray. Amen.

Declaration:
I have been crucified with Christ, and it's no longer
I who live but Christ who lives in me! The life I now
live in the flesh, I live by faith in the Son of Man
who gave Himself up for me. I walk in the Spirit and
do not gratify the desires of the flesh! God opens
my mouth with skillful and godly wisdom, and in
my tongue is the law of kindness. I have a tongue of
the learned and the wise. I know the word that sustains the weary, and I pray and speak in a way that
sets captives free. Jesus said that I would do even
greater works than He. I will start by sanctifying the
words of my mouth and by being passionate in
prayer. I am my Beloved's and He is mine. His
banner over me is love (see Galatians 2:20; Galatians 5:16; Proverbs 31:26; Isaiah 50:4; John 14:12).

what about you?

1. One of the great temptations for women is what I
   call "selective sharing." When we share the dirt on a
   particular woman with someone we know already
   dislikes her, that's selective sharing. When we've
   been bumped by a woman, and we share the news

with someone who has been shoved by her, that's selective sharing. When we selectively give information to someone to add weight to our criticism, that's selective sharing. What we don't realize is that we are poisoning our friend's perspective and making it harder for her to walk freely and with a pure heart. We are also adding to the weight of our own accountability. Read Ephesians 4:29 and ponder its meaning with regard to this issue. What is the uncommon thing to do? Write your thoughts.

2. Read Psalm 119:11. What sorts of things are hiding in your heart? In one way or another, they'll find their way out of your mouth. Rewrite this verse in your own words.

3. In the Old Testament we read account after account of how the (delivered) Israelites turned against Moses. They complained, they grumbled, and they gossiped. Moses was recorded to be the most humble man alive at the time. God wanted to destroy the wicked and petty people, but Moses placed himself between the people and God and interceded for them. Write about a time when your sincere efforts were met with suspicion. Describe how it felt.

4. Using the NIV, look up the following verses: Numbers 14:5; 16:4; 16:22; 16:45; and 20:6.

5. What was Moses and Aaron's consistent response in each of these situations? Why do you suppose they responded that way? Give some real thought to this and explain.

6. Read Exodus 33:11 and describe your thoughts and insights on why this relationship was so significant.

7. Write Luke 6:28 in prayer form, asking the Lord to transform you into His likeness.

the uncommon
woman changes
the world

*When we find ourselves trying
to avoid confronting some issue
in our life because of fear or dread or
wondering or reasoning, we should pray and
ask God to do for us what He has promised in His
Word—to go before us and pave the way for us.*[1]

⮾JOYCE MEYER

So do not fear, for I am with you; do not be
dismayed, for I am your God. I will strengthen
you and help you; I will uphold you with
my righteous right hand.

⮾ISAIAH 41:10

will not be bullied by her fears

I have a new friend who was horrifically abused as a child. Some of her stories have kept me awake at night. Unfortunately for the enemy, she is an overcomer. She has allowed God to take the ashes from her past and mold them into jewels fit for a crown. In the ways the enemy intended to destroy her, the Lord God Almighty has established her and is establishing her.

Restoration for her has come layer upon layer, memory upon memory. She, like all of us, has more healing to experience. But when I step back and look at how she has trusted God, and how He has filled her life with good things, I am challenged once again to remember *in my core* that God is who He says He is. He redeems. He restores. He delivers. And He establishes. When God is for us, who can ever successfully stand against us?

We all have a story to tell. And next month, we'll have more stories to tell. If we live by faith instead of being bullied by our fears, those stories will be ones of victory, inspiration, and triumph. Our stories will inspire others to put their fears under their feet.

The Bible says that we overcome the work of the enemy by the blood of the Lamb and the word of our testimony (see Revelation 12:11).

My friend has been saved and transformed because of the blood of the Lamb. She knows that it's the blood of Jesus poured out for her that allows her to live and forgive, and to love others. You could fill a whole book with her stories of faith and triumph.

And here's one such testimony. I received this wonderful e-mail from her:

There is something you must know about me; I am VERY claustrophobic. After being locked in bathrooms and closets and attacked in small areas, I do not do well in small places, busy crowds, or elevators. I am no way even near having a breakthrough in this area. But I have not had a panic attack since February. There is only one thing that challenges me to go beyond my fears . . . when I am challenged by my kids.

We were at the cabin with some friends, and they know I will not get in the boat if there are more than four people riding along. Also, when the kids are done wake boarding, tubing, and skiing, I feel much better if the extra adults get out of the boat.

The last time I went skiing with these particular friends, I crashed very hard and cut my bottom. It felt like I had given birth, and I peed lake water for three days. I vowed to never ski again. As we were getting into the boat, our friend asked if I was going to ski. "NO WAY!" I said. He replied, "If you put a wet suit on and you fall you won't feel a thing." Then my son Max piped in, "Yea, come on, Mom! This is going to be great! Mom's going skiing!" My little Max continued, "My mom can do anything. She is the best. Wait until you see my mom!"

I would not face the kids because I knew that the moment I put that tight wet suit on I was going to either panic or pass out. But darn it anyway, they always challenge me just by their own innocence and fearlessness.

They gave me the biggest suit so it wouldn't feel too snug for me. My husband, Rich, zipped up the back, and when it sucked my neck in I wanted out. I whispered, "I can't do this. It's way too tight."

Rich knows not to push me in this area so he was going to unzip it. But then my little Max came running down the dock and said, "Mom, if you get up I will wave and cheer for you when you come by the dock!!!" (UGH!!!!!!) (I was thinking, go away little kid.)

I stayed in the suit and grabbed the life jacket. When I finally put it on I thought I was going to pass out. I couldn't breathe and I was starting to hyperventilate. I sat in the boat and the only thing I could do was mentally challenge myself. I put my mind completely out there in this most fearful competitive state (like I used to do when I was a gymnast). As we were taking off in the boat my son yelled out, "Remember, Mom! If you're afraid, just do it anyway!" (Would someone shut this kid up?)

I got into the water. I couldn't move my feet because the skis were super tight. I couldn't breathe and I wanted to cry. I was terrified and felt trapped from my garments and trapped that I had to do this for my children.

I was in the water getting ready when I said a very unholy prayer. "God, I cannot make it one more minute in this suit, I am scared, my son bugs me, so please help me get up on these *dratted* skis the first time so I can get out of here."

Our friend hit the motor, and on my very first try I was up!!!!! I was skiing!!!!!! I started crying and I couldn't see a thing; I felt as if I was floating on the water. I was hanging on for dear life, and then I heard our friend honk as we went past the dock. I could hear cheers and clapping!!!! I made it more than halfway around the lake before I fell. I then wanted to make it back to the dock area, so I went for it again and I got up again! I let go of the rope by the dock and there was my son. He said for everyone to hear, "My mom is the best. She can do anything. Mom, you're the coolest mom ever. Your hair's even wet!"

I was bawling in the water, more out of relief that I didn't panic and black out. By the end of the weekend, my husband and I were skiing together at the same time. It was a small miracle but it was worth every wretched uncomfortable feeling I was experiencing. It truly was one of the hugest accomplishments of my life.

My eyes well up every time I read that story. To quote my pastor, "If that story doesn't stoke your fire, your wood is wet!"

My friend gritted her teeth, took on her fears, trusted God, and won the victory! From the world's standpoint, this woman has achieved some pretty amazing things—things most of us couldn't touch. Taking on her fear that day made all of heaven pause and watch and dance. Taking on our fears is a big, giant accomplishment.

⊚◎

What is fear anyway?

In the negative sense, fear is the feeling or the idea that something terrible might happen. Impending doom. Certain crisis. Painful rejection. Permanent loss. Worst-case scenarios.

When we are devastated or we hear about something terrible happening to someone else, those experiences mark us in a profound way (some more than others, depending on our own memories and experiences). If not dealt with, those fears can hold us captive. In my book *Alone in Marriage*, I wrote this about fear:

We all have a "pain pendulum" that compels us to react when we are first hurt in some way. Then, later on in life when situations arise that are remotely reminiscent to our initial memory, we tend to overreact and overcompensate, and our beliefs are once again confirmed that people and circumstances (and sometimes God) cannot be trusted.

Until we are willing to dig beneath the surface and reconcile our wrong beliefs and fears with the wonderful truths of God, we will be held captive by our past experiences. Unless we deal with our fears, the beliefs about our painful past experiences will continue to hurt us because they will continually translate into current wrong beliefs.[2]

Satan is a ruthless being, and he will attempt to threaten us all day long. But thankfully, there's *always* God. Since we in ourselves are no match for the devil, he will try—in our most vulnerable moments—to get away with making our knees knock and our hearts race. But in every situation, we must remember God.

"My flesh and my heart may fail, but God is the strength of my heart and my portion forever" (Psalm 73:26).

Jesus has made provision for our weakness, and He understands our fears. That's where His glory shines the most. He steps into our low and desperate places and, with a grand smile and a powerful right hand, He lifts us up and proves Himself faithful again and again.

For the longest time I lived in fear of the future. Since God allowed some terrible things to happen to me (and because He allows horrific things to happen to others), I constantly feared that the next battle would be *the* over-the-top trial; the one that was sure to take me out of commission. People often say that God won't give you more than you can handle, but . . . At the risk of sounding too cynical, that's tough to hear when you're the one who feels you're about to be crushed under the load of it all. After all, even Paul said he was "hard pressed on every side, but not crushed . . . struck down, but not destroyed" (2 Corinthians 4:8–9). We can only bear what we're given because of the strength of God!

During the worst part of my journey I used to clench my fists and yell out loud, "God! I think You have me mixed up with a Susie Larson in Cincinnati. Because this is much more than *I* can handle!"

And yet, now that I am on the other side of some of those wretched battles, I stand in awe. I finally realize in the very core of my being that I would not be the person I am today if not for the struggles God allowed me to endure.

With all my heart I now know that Jesus understands how transient I am. He knows I am but dust. He knows which battles will take me out and which ones will strengthen me. *He* is the One who can and will keep me from falling. *He* is the One who will present me before God's glorious presence *without fault* and *with great joy* (see Jude 24). You can know for certain that He is carefully guarding His treasure.

When we stay within the bounds He has set for us and when we dwell in His presence, we will be safe there. With boldness we can face our future battles and proclaim, "I will survive this, and I will thrive because of it! Every battle God allows me to endure is a winnable one! I am daily being made into His image, and I can trust Him!"

When I consider the work God has done in my own heart, my knees get weak and I spill over with love and gratitude all over again. That He would take on this awkward, fearful creature and turn me into someone He can use proves that He is intent on delivering each and every one of us from all that holds us captive. He sets us free that we might work alongside Him to set others free.

Though the enemy has been given access to this world through the choices of man, his doom is certain. Though he is allowed to devastate people on a very deep level, he *never* wins against the believer. It may seem he's won for a season, but he hasn't. He wins a few skirmishes, but he already knows he has lost the war.

As long as we remember who we are and *whose* we are, we will walk, breathe, and live with the knowledge that Jesus makes all things new. When we hold on to faith and stand on God's Word, we can reclaim the abundant life the enemy has tried to steal from us. Furthermore, when we learn more about our promised rights as a believer, we won't give the devil such open access to rob us blind.

Like my friend in the opening story, God will allow us to have a face-off with our fears because He knows that with Him at our side, we can win in our confrontations with fear. What's wonderful is that every time we face a fear and recover something the enemy has tried to keep from us, *our appetite for freedom* increases. And it's *for* freedom that Christ has set us free. Stand firm then, and refuse to be enslaved by your fears.

"It is for freedom that Christ has set us free. Stand firm, then, and do not let yourselves be burdened again by a yoke of slavery" (Galatians 5:1).

How many choices do you suppose we've made out of fear; choices that sabotage our victory and the abundant life to which we were called? Out of fear, we as God's people have . . .

- ❖ *Broken off relationships that seemed too good to be true because we didn't want to get hurt.*
- ❖ *Contemplated suicide because death seemed more hopeful than life.*
- ❖ *Started a fight because we thought the other person might strike first.*
- ❖ *Said no to a certain job or opportunity because we were afraid to fail.*

❖ *Said no to visiting another country because we were afraid of travel.*

❖ *Said no to trying something new because we were afraid of what others might think.*

❖ *Prolonged misery because we were too afraid to make a tough decision.*

❖ *Gone way into debt because we didn't trust the Lord deeply.*

For us to be the uncommon women God has called us to be, we have to face our fears. Not that we should go carelessly running into traffic in the hopes that Jesus will rescue us before the traffic clobbers us. Jesus isn't asking us to run haphazardly toward the things that scare us half to death. That would be silly. But are we willing to step out in faith *when God calls us to something new?* Can we humbly and honestly give God permission (in His own way and in His own time) to deliver us from the evil lies that imprison us?

Most of what we fear will never happen. Yet we destroy our joy and interrupt our journey just in case there's the tiniest, remotest possibility that they will. We have to love God more than our fears.

Our life is a message. Everything we do, and say, and pray speaks a message to the world and to God. Even the things we don't do send a message. In their book *The Making of a Spiritual Warrior*, authors Quin Sherrer and Ruthanne Garlock wrote:

> Fear. Dread. Alarm. Some women live in such perpetual fear, especially for their children or husbands. Fear can be beneficial when it warns us of impending danger, but when taken to extremes and coupled with worry, it quickly becomes a heavy bondage. If we Christian women allow fear to dominate our thoughts, we're really telling God we don't trust him. We don't mean to send that message, but somehow we have gotten so caught up in fearful worry, we don't realize the depth of our bondage.[3]

Just what are we to do about our fears? Is it possible to take them all on at once? I don't think so. God can, if He so chooses, to supernaturally deliver us in a moment's time, and sometimes He does. But just as often, He tells us to put one foot in front of the other and follow His lead; and in doing so, He shows us our moment-by-moment need for Him. That way we learn how to trust; we learn how to battle.

One morning I sat out on my deck, hugged my morning cup of coffee, and listened to the morning birds sing their song. Rays of light beamed through the trees, and all at once I was having church in my outdoor sanctuary.

"So, Lord," I prayed, "what am I to do with all of this fear and anxiety I am feeling?" His answer came to me as clear as the morning dew glimmering on the trees: *Walk in My authority. Rest in My care.*

His words poured over me like fresh falling rain. I opened my hands in my lap and just sat there a little while longer. I had spent months learning about the authority we as believers have in Christ. I had spent many more months learning the powerful lesson of *living* from a place of rest. That's why this simple state-ment meant so much to me. It was packed with meaning.

Though I had learned (for the most part), to live from a place of rest, rest left me whenever fear reared its ugly head. And though the level of authority God has entrusted to His children has had a profound impact on me, I'd often go quickly from victor to victim when I was threatened by my fears.

Amazing how we let go of what we know when we're afraid, no? Well, I am going to give you a powerful tool to help you hold on to the authority you have in Christ Jesus.

In the fabulous devotional *Sparkling Gems from the Greek,* author Rick Renner shows us what it looks like to stand against the lies of the enemy. He tells us that the devil's primary goal is to get into a person's mind and fill it with lying emotions, false perceptions, and confusion. He then references 2 Corinthians 10:5 where we are told to bring every inferior thought into captivity. Read this powerful excerpt from his book:

> The words "bringing into captivity" are from the Greek word *aichmalotidzo*, which pictured *a soldier who had captured an enemy and now leads him into captivity with the point of a sharpened spear thrust into the flesh in his back*. The captured enemy knows that if he tries to move or get away, the Roman soldier will shove that spear clear through his torso and kill him. Therefore, this captive doesn't dare move but remains silent, submissive, and nonresistant.
>
> However, when Paul uses the word *aichmalotidzo* in this verse, he writes in a tense that describes the *continuous action* of taking such an enemy captive. This is not a one-time affair; it is the lifelong occupation of the soldier. . . . Because the devil loves to make a playground out of your mind and emotions, you must deal with him like a real enemy. Rather than fall victim to the devil's attacks, you must make a mental decision to seize every thought he tries to use to penetrate your mind and emotions. Rather than let those thoughts take you captive, you have to reach up and grab them and *force* them into submission! You must take *every* thought captive to the obedience of Christ![4]

Wherever you go, Jesus is there with you. Remember, when you walk into a room the spiritual climate changes because you belong to the Most High God and He has assigned angels to your care. You are someone He loves and wants to protect. Know what you possess in Christ. Read the Bible and learn what God says about *who you are*. You are never out from His watchful eye, and when you spend much time dwelling in His presence, you will learn to *rest* there. She who spends much time in the secret place of the Most High God will learn how to live and rest in His shadow. If you continually struggle with fear, spend a significant amount of time in Psalm 91 and get a firm grasp of the provision and the protection God offers those who look to Him.

      ㈲

"Much-Afraid," said the Shepherd again, "tell me, what is the matter. Why were you so fearful?"

"It is the way you have chosen for me to go," she whispered. "It looks so dreadful, Shepherd, so impossible. I turn giddy and faint whenever I look at it. The roes and hinds go there, but they are not limping, crippled, or cowardly like me."

"But, Much-Afraid, what did I promise you in the Valley of Humiliation?" asked the Shepherd with a smile.

Much-Afraid looked startled, and the blood rushed into her cheeks and ebbed again, leaving them as white as before. "You said," she began and broke off and then began again, "O Shepherd, you said you would make my feet like hinds' feet and set me upon mine High Places."

"Well," he answered cheerfully, "the only way to develop hinds' feet is to go by the paths which the hinds use—like this one." Much-Afraid trembled and looked at him shamefacedly. "I don't think—I want—hinds' feet, if it means I have to go on a path like that," she said slowly and painfully.

"Oh, yes you do," he said cheerfully. "I know you better than you know yourself, Much-Afraid. You want it very much indeed, and I promise you these hinds feet . . . I don't know anything more delightful than turning weakness into strength, and fear into faith, and that which has been marred into perfection."[5]

We were made for the high places. We are equipped to thrive in the low places. We have all that we need to take out the giants in our land. God is bigger than any problem we can face. And we please Him by our faith.

Uncommon woman, refuse to be bullied by your fears. Determine to fulfill every last thing He had in mind for you when He created you. Be the woman He intended you to be. Don't obey your fears. Obey Him instead.

I've chosen a few swords for you to take along your way. Pick up each one and get a feel for it. Learn how and when to use each of these weapons of your warfare. Above all, remind yourself, every single day, that *you* are the object of His affection. He thinks you are perfectly wonderful, and His perfect love will cast out every fear. Let His love fill up your heart and mind, and take the place of every lesser thing.

Now pick up your sword. . . .

His grace is sufficient for me! His power works best in my weakness! (See 2 Corinthians 12:9.)

Greater is He that is in me than He that is in the world. (See 1 John 4:4.)

I have been crucified with Christ and it's no longer I who live, but Christ who lives in me, and the life I now live in the flesh, I live by faith in the Son of God who loved me and gave Himself up for me. (See Galatians 2:20.)

I can do all things through Christ who strengthens me. (See Philippians 4:13.)

God has not given me a spirit of fear, but of power, and of love, and of a sound mind. (See 2 Timothy 1:7.)

Overwhelming victory is mine in Christ Jesus. (See Romans 8:37.)

I am more than a conqueror because of Christ. (See Romans 8:37.)

I can block every fiery dart the devil sends my way, simply by raising my shield of faith. (See Ephesians 6:16.)

God gives me His shield of victory; His right hand sustains me; He stoops down to make me great. (See Psalm 18:35.)

God goes before me and behind me and He places His hand of blessing on my head. (See Psalm 139:5.)

I will trust in God and I will not be afraid! (See Psalm 56:4, 11; and Psalm 118:6.)

> *The soul loves and is loved in return; she seeks and is sought; she calls and is called. But in this, she lifts and is lifted up; she holds and is herself held; she clasps and she is closely embraced, and by the bond of love she unites herself to God, one with one, alone with Him.*[6]
>
> SAINT THOMAS AQUINAS

Want the cure for fear? It's simple. Intimacy with God.

Precious Lord,
You are my dearest Friend. There is no one like You.
Though my fears are many, Your love is greater than
all of them. I will, by faith, press through the things
that scare me that I might lay hold of all You have
promised me. You've made me for the high places.
You've appointed me for victory. It pleases You to see
me conquer fear. Fill me up once again with more of
You. Increase my capacity to comprehend Your perfect
love. Your precious, perfect love casts out every fear,
every foe, and every defeating thought. I say this today,
out loud for everyone to hear: I will serve You, and not
my fears. By the power of Your great name, I pray.
Amen.

Declaration:

In Jesus' Name I declare that I can do all things through Christ who strengthens me! I refuse fear and embrace faith instead. I will no longer be bullied by my fears because God has great things for me to do! My eyes are on Him and my ears are tuned to His voice. I will listen to Jesus and not to the threats of the enemy. I refuse every lying voice and fearful thought that the enemy sends my way. In fact, I will put those thoughts into captivity with the sword of the Spirit. I will not give them an inch of land or a moment of my time! I will embrace thoughts consistent with God's Word, and I know that I will triumph! Overwhelming victory is mine because I am in Christ!

what about you?

1. In the Gospels we read about the woman with the issue of blood. She had a horrible life. She was no doubt exhausted from the constant loss of blood. She probably dealt with the humiliation of chronic body odor. As a woman who was bleeding, she was most likely shunned by society. Hers was a life of desperation. With this picture in mind, consider your fears as something that diminishes your ability to enjoy life; keeps you from living out your God-given calling. Read Luke 8:40–48 and write down your thoughts.

2. Write out your own prayer, asking God to bring you to a new level of freedom in your walk of faith.

3. Joyce Meyer says that fear stands for "False Evidence Appearing Real." Read what Jesus has to say about the devil in John 8:44; then write down the ways you have been deceived by him in the past. What did you learn from those times? Explain.

4. Read Isaiah 54:4 and write it out in a personalized prayer from God to you. Remember, He loves you and wants to protect and restore you.

*A spiritual kingdom lies all
about us, enclosing us, embracing
us, altogether within reach of our inner
selves, waiting for us to recognize it. God
Himself is here awaiting our response to His
presence. This eternal world will come alive to us
the moment we begin to reckon upon its reality.*[1]

&A. W. TOZER

Therefore, since we are surrounded by such a huge
crowd of witnesses to the life of faith, let us strip off
every weight that slows us down, especially the sin
that so easily trips us up. And let us run with
endurance the race that God has set before us.

&HEBREWS 12:1 NLT

believes
His promises
are true

"Tell me about the most amazing God-moment you've ever experienced. What story has inspired you to faith more than any other?"

One of our church leaders asked this question as we sat around the table and shared a meal with a missionary who was visiting our church. Mervus (the missionary) spoke up and said, "I have one; it's about my mentor." (I'll call Mervus's mentor James since I can't remember his name. I was so captivated with the story that his name came and left before I had the chance to grab hold of it.)

Mervus continued. "James is the most amazing man of faith I have ever met. He *knows* what he possesses in Christ. It's like he brings an increased sense of God's presence with him wherever he goes. His understanding of the promises and the purposes of God surpasses anyone I know.

"James was invited to Africa to minister to some missionaries there. The people felt depressed and oppressed and couldn't seem to get out from under the dark cloud that had descended upon them. They were desperate for James to arrive.

"The plane landed on the tarmac in Africa, and when the door of the plane opened, a man was standing there waiting to meet James. The host weakly grabbed James's hand and said, 'Brother James, we're so glad you are here. We've been so depressed, brother James. Now that you're here, can you feel the darkness and oppression in this land?'"

With a pregnant pause, excited to tell us the best part of the story, Mervus leaned in and said, "James stepped onto the tarmac, looked this man square in the eye, and said, 'You listen here. I have the living, powerful God of heaven alive in my soul. When I step foot on this land, *that* oppression feels *me*.'"

This story about knocked me over. I sat back in my chair and imagined the exchange between these two men. Under my breath, I whispered a prayer. *I must have more of You, Lord.*

A little disclaimer here: This is not to say that we are defective disciples if we come upon times of oppression when we need someone to loan us their faith in order to help us stand. In fact, I walked through such a time while writing this book. We need each other on this journey of faith.

However, Mervus's story challenges us to more firmly, more resolutely walk out my life verse: "And so I walk in the Lord's presence as I live here on earth!" (Psalm 116:9 NLT). God's presence is bursting with promises, provision, and protection. And when we lay hold of, in an ever-increasing way, what we possess in Christ, we will believe (*as we should*) that everywhere we place our feet, God's Kingdom comes to bear.

Uncommon woman, when you keep Jesus on the throne of your life every—single—day, and when you determine to be done with attitudes and activities that are beneath you, you will be positioned to march into your next place of promise.

You know, the Israelites took forty years to take a journey

that should only have taken them a week or two. Many scholars say that the delayed journey was a direct result of their rebellious fears and unbelief.

"The people refused to enter the pleasant land, for they wouldn't believe his promise to care for them. Instead, they grumbled in their tents and refused to obey the Lord" (Psalm 106:24–25 NLT).

They refused to believe the Promise, and then they grumbled because their lives had no promise. Before we come down too hard on the Israelites, we need to look in the mirror. I cringe when I think of how many times I've grumbled because I didn't even consider bringing my need to my gracious Father who loves to give good gifts to His children.

Do you know why God absolutely detests grumbling and complaining? Because God is the source of all things and *we* are the object of His affection! The Lord is our Shepherd and we shall not want. God has promised to meet all of our needs according to *His* riches. The Bible says that all of God's promises are "Yes" and "Amen" (2 Corinthians 1:20)! He is and has everything we need. When we stay within the shelter of His loving care, He will more than meet our needs. God is not a respecter of persons, but He is a respecter of faith.

> His divine power has given us everything we need for life and god-liness through our knowledge of him who called us by his own glory and goodness. Through these he has given us his very great and precious promises, so that through them you may participate in the divine nature and escape the corruption in the world caused by evil desires. (2 Peter 1:3–4)

Divine power—everything you need for life and godliness. Great promises, precious promises, so that through them, you can—every single day—participate in *His Divine nature*. The more you know Him, the more you'll love Him. And the more you love Him, the more you'll trust Him and believe what He says. This is the powerful, uncommon life.

The Israelites' journey parallels our journey. *They* were not made for captivity. *We* were not made for captivity. *They* were made to live free and reign as representatives of the Most High God. *We* were made to live free and reign as representatives of the Most High God.

We live in captivity when we lose sight of our destiny. We won't take hold of God's promises if we don't believe they are true for us. The enemy's greatest desire is to get us to doubt the goodness and the honor of God, because then we will let go of expectancy and faith and hope and love. And then we will get comfortable in our captivity and make our own idols. As uncommon women, we are called to press on from one place of victory to the next, from one promise to the next, from one level of faith and hope and love, to the next.

What you do matters. What you say matters. If you pray, it matters. And if you choose to live a life without faith, it matters very much.

Without faith it is *impossible* to please God. Think about that. You can't make Him happy if your unbelief always trumps your faith. He'll still love you, but you won't awaken His pleasure. He's done so much for you, and He wants to do *even more* in and through you.

When you come upon a difficult time, consider it a grand opportunity to make Him smile. Say to yourself, *Normally my tendency would be to get tied up in a knot over this, but I am going to look to Jesus instead. As I prayerfully bring my need before Him, and I thank Him ahead of time for His answer, I will be twice blessed. I will find peace while I wait, and I will get to see firsthand how God wants to work in my life!*

What we do with the promises of God will affect how we

relate to our friends, our enemies, our husbands, our children, and the lonely woman who lives down the block. How we view our responsibility in light of what God has offered us will have a direct impact on how we contribute to the life of our church, our community, and the poor.

When the abundant promise of provision gets under our skin, we just have to make a difference in our world. In ourselves, it's natural and easy to pick apart our coworkers, and our church and government leaders. We could do it better, right? And yet, as the reality of God's Kingdom grows within us, our passion to become part of the solution (rather than cynically spout about the problem) increases as well. And you can make quite a difference in the world when you have access to the riches of heaven. You *can* make a difference, and you *do* have access.

Unbelief neglects the spiritual soil. Belief prepares for rain. Think about it. A farmer believes so much in this crazy notion of growth and harvest that he turns over the soil, removes the rocks, and plants his seed. He guards his investment by keeping out the weeds and the small animals that threaten to devour his harvest. He sets himself up for success.

If we don't believe God's promises are true for us in this day, we will pay little attention to our bad attitudes and behaviors. Our feet will be crusted with dirt, but that won't bother us so much because everyone else, at least that we can see, has more dirt on their feet than we do on ours. Our heart's soil might be a bit hardened, but for good reason, right?

If we don't believe God's promises are true, we will give the enemy's lies free rein in our brain as if those lies are just little irritants and not some kind of deadly poison. We wonder why our spiritual lives are lethargic, and yet without knowing it, we have poisoned ourselves.

If we don't believe God's promises are true for us today, we will think nothing of taking care of our problems in the way we always have: with our own understanding and the thirty-two bucks we have in our wallet. We will live earthbound lives with little hope, small faith, and conditional love.

Some Christians think that all of the good stuff is supposed to happen on the other side, when we get to heaven. But not here. Not now. Wrong!

Search the Scriptures for yourself, and soak in all of the promises that are yours for the taking! You will see the goodness of the Lord in the land of the living! He is able to make loads of grace abound to you in all times and in all ways so that you may abound in every good work! He came that we might have life and have it more abundantly! He made us for *continual* increase, a multiplied return on His investment, and to bear much fruit. And do you know when all of this became possible for you? The day you said yes to Him.

We are called to go from strength to strength, from victory to victory, shining ever brighter until the full light of day (see Psalm 84:7; Proverbs 4:18). Depending on our season of life, the temptation will be present to choose *anything* else but faith. During times of abundance, the temptation will be to shift our weight off of faith and onto our finances. During times of health, it will be to rely on our own strength, and thus loosen our grip of the Vine. During times of prominence in position, we may find it easy to think we're really something and thus forget that we are really nothing without Him.

Abundant times are as much a test of our faith as the valley times. Success will test our hearts and ask the question, "Are you still holding on to Jesus first and foremost? Do you still believe that it's His grace that got you here? Are you humbly grateful because you know that a thousand people could take your place?"

And then there are the valleys. Do we camp in the valleys or contend with them? Tomorrow or the next day or sometime in the near future you will need to pack up your bag of comforts and march forward to your next place of promise with faith in your heart and Jesus at your side.

"And without faith it is impossible to please God, because anyone who comes to him must believe that he exists and that he rewards those who earnestly seek him" (Hebrews 11:6). We are called "believers" because we believe. But do we really? As believers we are called to progressively grow in our capacity to *believe*. This requires a continual willingness to *seek*. But in seeking Him there is great *reward*! Read the verse above again. And again.

The common Christian approaches faith sitting down. She watches as interesting people pass her by, and she wonders what it would be like to be one of them. The sameness of her life bores her yet makes her feel secure all at the same time. If something's out of reach, she thinks it's not for her, because she is, after all, sitting down.

And yet, the believer's life is supposed to be one *standing* on the promises, *moving* in the power of the Holy Spirit, and *reaching* for the impossible because God is with her. The uncommon woman's call is to a life of conquests, victories, and humble obedience to the Lord's leading. Oswald Chambers wrote, "If we are eating only out of our own hand, and doing things solely on our own initiative without expecting God to come in, we are on a downward path. We have lost our vision."[2]

Your new "land" might consist of turning your back on a fear that has been crippling you and choosing instead to embrace the God who will deliver you. Or maybe your new conquest involves taking on a project that is way over your head and beyond your natural ability to accomplish, and yet God is calling you onward.

Your next place of promise might be as sweet as enjoying peace-filled nights with deeper sleep and less anxiety. Stepping out for you might be in your willingness to give away a large sum of money to the poor. Or maybe you're being compelled to say yes to a request that makes your knees weak and your heart race.

One way or the other, you are called to faith—the stretching, reaching, I don't-know-if-I-can-do-this kind of faith. And when you shift all of your hopes and dreams into the arms of the Most High God, you will find Him faithful. It's *impossible* for a woman to be everything she is called to be without radical, powerful, out-on-a-limb kind of belief in the promises and the person of Jesus Christ. Exercise your faith. Nurture it. Practice it. Believe His promises are true, because they are.

And remember, we can extinguish *every* fiery dart that comes our way by raising up our shield of faith (see Ephesians 6:16).

What we do with the promises of God is the tipping point in every area of our lives. Whether or not we decide to believe that we have access to the very power that raised Christ from the dead will determine just how uncommon our lives turn out to be.

Though we will have trials, His promises are true. Though we may not feel Him at times, He is still there. And though the enemy would love for us to settle for less, God gets absolutely giddy when we reach for more.

Graham Cooke wrote this wonderful insight:

There is an inheritance and favor over your life right now. God has a continuous stream of blessing for you that He wants to release—if you are not presently living in it, you are robbing yourself of incredible joy. We are called to inherit this blessing for ourselves, and for everyone around us. What if the promise of God in your life was so large that it could cover ten square blocks in your community? Wouldn't you want to know what that blessing is? God is extravagant and lavish enough to do that—and much more.[3]

Don't settle. Lay hold of everything God has made available

to you that you might make the biggest impact possible in your world. Don't put more faith in your obstacles than you do the promises of God. Don't give more credence to your limitations than you do to God's unlimited capacity to intervene.

Live a life of faith.

A number of years ago I felt compelled to spend much of my devotional time in Romans 4. For months I pondered Paul's account of Abraham's faith, which was absolutely staggering to me.

Abraham's body was old and as good as dead. And though he faced that fact, he *didn't weaken* in his faith. In fact, he was *strengthened* in his faith; you know why? Because he only gave his limitations a passing look, so he could *gaze* at the One who to him was a Promise Keeper. Abraham was *convinced* that God was true and would come through for him.

After much time pondering the powerful faith of this amazing man, I wrote my own personalized prayer adapted from Romans 4 and a few other verses. I share it with you now, my uncommon and faith-filled friend. Make it your own and march on to your next place of promise.

> *God is looking for those with whom He can do the impossible. What a pity that we plan only the things we can do by ourselves!*
>
> A. W. TOZER

Without weakening in my faith

I will face the FACT that there are many reasons

I should not be able to fulfill the call on my life

BUT I will not waiver in unbelief regarding the promises of God!

No! I will be strengthened in my faith, giving glory to God

Because I am FULLY persuaded that

GOD has the power and is able to do what He has promised

Therefore I will put no confidence in my flesh, or my abilities, or even my obstacles

But I will put ALL of my hope in the power and the dignity and the love

Of Almighty God

Who loves me and DAILY establishes His purposes for me!

Hallelujah!

What we do affects today and tomorrow. We are that important. What will you do with the promises offered you?

Faithful Father,
You've been so good to me. Forgive me for the times
I've chosen fear and unbelief over faith and hope. You
are my richest treasure, and I possess all in You. Help
me to live above and not beneath my circumstances.
Help me to function from a place of overflow and not
emptiness. Open my eyes to really see who I am in You,
and who You are to me. I know this isn't about doing
more, but rather "being more" with You. When I abide
closely to the Vine, I bear much fruit. Keep me close
enough to feel Your heartbeat and to hear Your voice. I
am Yours and You are mine. Your promises are true and
You will make a way for me. I believe this with my
whole heart. Amen.

Declaration:
In Jesus' Name I declare that I can do all things through Christ who strengthens me! Daily my capacity for faith increases; daily I gain more clarity about my calling, and daily I walk in His presence as

I live here on earth! I walk in the Spirit, and I do not gratify the desires of the flesh. My heart is set on the Lord, and I live the way He wants me to live. God is good, His promises are true, and He will make a way for me. I will not commit the sin of unbelief! Amen.

what about you?

1. Read Matthew 7:7 and write down these three things:

   • What things are you asking the Lord for today?

   • In what ways are you seeking after intimacy with God?

   • In what ways are you knocking, or inquiring of the Lord (in other words, what are you searching out that you might understand Him more)?

2. Read Matthew 7:8 and think about your level of expectancy. As you review your three points above, are you more "expectant" in one area than another? Write down a prayer asking God to increase your capacity for faith and expectancy.

3. Read Matthew 7:9–11 and ask yourself these questions, "Do I believe that God is a good Father? Is there any discrepancy between what the Word says

about Him and what I think of Him?" Explain. If your answer is yes, make this a point of prayer. Seek until you find Him to be just who He says He is. If your answer is no, simply write a prayer thanking God for your capacity to know Him.

4. Read Matthew 7:12 and consider the reason this verse is found just after this magnificent call to belief. In what ways are you affecting the world around you? Write them down. Now spend some quiet time with the Lord and dare to ask Him to give you a God-sized vision for your life. Buckle your seat belt.

*The stronghold of God is not only a
place to visit God but to dwell with Him.
For those who dwell with God, His presence
is not merely our refuge; it is a permanent address.*[1]

❧ FRANCIS FRANGIPANE

God is bedrock under my feet, the castle in which I live,
my rescuing knight. . . . The Lord is my rock, my fortress,
and my savior; my God is my rock, in whom I find
protection. He is my shield, the power that
saves me, and my place of safety.

❧ PSALM 18:2A THE MESSAGE; PSALM 18:2 NLT

chapter eleven

stays in the stronghold of God

"I used to struggle with pornography," a man once candidly told me.

"How did you get through it all?" I asked.

"God revealed something to me that forever changed the way I think about His protection."

"Tell me!" I said.

The man continued. "I'm someone who takes my walk of faith seriously. I love Jesus, and I hated myself for struggling with such an insidious sin. I begged God for strength, for forgiveness, and then for strength again. One day God showed me a picture of a strong, stone wall that surrounded and protected my life. It was beautiful, except one part of the wall was broken down, leaving my life open to the influences of the enemy. I was instantly convicted of the kinds of movies I watch (not pornographic, but suggestive), and for surfing the Internet during work hours (again, not looking at pornography but wasting time when I should have been working).

"Deep inside I knew these things were wrong, but I justified them because I know lots of other Christians who were doing the same thing. What I hadn't realized was that by making these compromises with media, I opened myself up for much worse things. I was the one who broke down the wall so I could reach out and grab the things I wanted, and in doing so, I opened myself up to sin that could have destroyed every good thing in my life. I confessed those sins, I've risen to the standard Christ has set for me, I've reinforced my wall, and now I enjoy living a powerful and peaceful life within the stronghold of God."

I loved that illustration. We break down *our own* wall of protection when we reach for what isn't ours and when we do what God has asked us not to do. This story perfectly expresses why God has set certain boundaries in place for us. Some consider Christianity a long list of dos and don'ts that make us weird and irrelevant to the rest of the world. But that's *not* Christianity; what they are describing, as you may know, is religion, not relationship.

Our Heavenly Protector has laid out boundaries for us, but not because He's an angry, sterile God who doesn't know how to have fun. On the contrary, *He's* the One who invented laughter, sunny days, and cliff jumping.

Our loving Father put certain boundaries in place because He wants our lives fortified against all of the schemes of the enemy. He is a colorful, beautiful, hilarious God, but He hates what the enemy wants to do to us.

❧

My husband and I have three grown sons. Though we've made our share of mistakes, we have tried to parent them the way God has parented us. We clearly communicated where their boundaries began and where they ended. We let our boys know about the consequences that awaited them should they decide to take wisdom into their own hands and venture out beyond where our arms could reach them.

We also let them know how great life could be and would be if they stayed within the age-appropriate boundaries we had set for them. When they made the right choices, we blessed them like crazy. When they stepped outside their borders, we let them experience the consequences. We wanted them to get a feel for Kingdom living.

They, like most kids, have done their share of venturing out, but for the most part, they've enjoyed a blessed and wonderful life. My middle son Luke used to be my strong-willed one (he is now a gentle giant with a David-like heart for worship). He used to spend more time in the corner than not. I remember one day when he was headed to his room for a little time-out. He stepped in his room and shut the door. Seconds later he poked his head back out and said, "I think I'm starting to get this. Good choices, good life. Bad choices, bad life."

I had to suppress my laughter until he closed the door again. Now I am not suggesting that life is that much of a cliché, but in the general sense, Luke makes a good point.

We are uncommon women. We are called to do great things and live in a noble way. God wants to expand His Kingdom in us and through us. We were made for a beautiful, abundant life. But there's a small problem. We have feet of clay and a sin nature that longs to dominate our lives.

The *only* way we can ever hope to make the kinds of choices that translate into the powerful lives we were destined for is to *live* under the shelter of the Most High. It's to *walk* in the Spirit and not gratify the desires of the flesh. It's to *stay* so connected to the Vine that when considering our choices we are willing to say, "If I have to let go of Him to take hold of that, then I don't want it. If I can't reach it while hanging on to the Vine, then it's not for me."

To continually and instinctively take the high road requires that we live close enough to God that we feel His heartbeat. When our heart beats in rhythm with His, we begin to feel the way He does. Over time we develop a distaste for that which diminishes life, and we develop a divine hunger for that which nourishes the soul.

Just how do we stay under the shelter and make it our *permanent address* as in Francis Frangipane's words from the beginning of this chapter? Three things: 1.) We trust; 2.) We obey; 3.) We live as one who is spoken for. And what do we gain as a result? Read on:

"Praise be to the God and Father of our Lord Jesus Christ, who has blessed us in the heavenly realms with every spiritual blessing in Christ" (Ephesians 1:3).

We trust

Would you stand under a bridge in a rainstorm if you thought it might come crashing down on you? No, you would rather take your chances with the thunder and the lightning.

If we don't absolutely trust the goodness and faithfulness of God, we will repeatedly step out from under His protection by taking matters into our own hands. We sometimes take our chances on the very things that could destroy us. And then we *miss out* on the blessedness of having God hide us in the shadow of His wing.

Proverbs 9:10 says, "Knowledge of the Holy One is understanding." The more we get to know Jesus, the more we will understand why He guides us the way He does. When we understand that His motivation is always for our highest good, we will *trust* Him even when we don't understand Him. He deserves all of our trust and so much more.

"Trust in the Lord with all your heart; do not depend on your own understanding. Seek his will in all you do, and he will show you which path to take" (Proverbs 3:5–6 NLT).

"The Lord is my strength and shield. I trust him with all my heart. He helps me, and my heart is filled with joy. I burst out in songs of thanksgiving" (Psalm 28:7 NLT).

When the ground shakes beneath your feet or circumstances rock your world, say out loud for your own ears to hear, "I will trust You, Lord! I will not be afraid!" When slanderous words find their way to your ears, proclaim out loud, "You are the One who defines me, Lord! I will trust Your opinion far and above anyone else's!"

When temptation feels like it's lassoed your ankle, declare, "You are my stronghold and my Deliverer! You will lift me up out of this trap! I will trust You to keep me in the shadow of Your wings!" And when the frantic pace of life pulls you down its current, and it seems there's no rest in sight for you, look up and say, "You will lead me beside still waters. You allow me to lie down in green pastures. You will keep me in perfect peace when I keep my eyes on You. I will trust You to lead me to a place of divine rest."

He can be trusted. In fact, it's amazing He even allows us to have such a debate. He has been faithful through the ages. He's gone the distance to show us He loves us. And though we remember on Tuesday that He can be trusted, but then forget again on Wednesday, He stands with an open hand, waiting to lead us back to a right perspective and a peaceful heart. What an amazingly kind God He is.

♋

We obey

"But for you who obey me, my saving power will rise on you like the sun and bring healing like the sun's rays. You will be as free and happy as calves let out of a stall" (Malachi 4:2 GNT).

Read the verse from Malachi again. Do you see what I see? Obedience doesn't imprison us, it sets—us—free.

God's provision protects us (we won't have to venture out on our own; He will more than meet our needs).

His wisdom warns us (we will know the difference between right and wrong; He will keep us from falling).

And His peace leads us (we can know which way to go; He goes before us).

When God whispers to our hearts, *Make the call*, or *Send the card*, or *Forgive her*, we obey. When our stubbornness rises up within us and we want to react with pride and anger, we remember the basin, we remember humility, and we obey by putting those reactive attitudes under our feet so they won't get spewed into someone's face.

When we feel like spending money we don't have, or saying things we shouldn't say, we take sides against ourselves and we do the right thing.

We find the strength to live this uncommon life by our direct connection to the Source of all that's right and good. Each time we respond in humble obedience to the circumstances God entrusts to us, we are strengthened in faith and matured in love. We are not called to "be perfect" by ourselves, but to be perfectly joined to the One who can make us like Him.

When we spend much time in the secret place with God, we get to know His voice and His ways. And when we come to value His voice in our lives (above all else), we will do what He says because we know He speaks from a higher perspective. And when we follow His lead and do as He does, we will find ourselves *living* under the shelter of the Most High God.

Psalm 91

Those who live in the shelter of the Most High will find rest in the shadow of the Almighty. This I declare of the Lord: he alone is my refuge, my place of safety; he is my God, and I trust him. For he will rescue you from every trap and protect you from deadly disease. He will cover you with his feathers. He will shelter you with his wings. His faithful promises are your armor and protection. Do not be afraid of the terrors of the night, nor the arrow that flies in the day. Do not dread the disease that stalks in darkness, nor the disaster that strikes at midday. Though a thousand fall at your side, though ten thousand are dying around you, these evils will not touch you. Just open your eyes, and see how the wicked are punished. If you make the Lord your refuge, if you make the Most High your shelter, no evil will conquer you; no plague will come near your home. For he will order his angels to protect you wherever you go. They will hold you up with their hands so you won't even hurt your foot on a stone. You will trample upon lions and cobras; you will crush fierce lions and serpents under your feet! The Lord says, "I will rescue those who love me. I will protect those who trust in my name. When they call on me, I will answer; I will be with them in trouble. I will rescue them and honor them. I will reward them with a long life and give them my salvation."

Nature obeys Him—it doesn't have a choice. Evil spirits obey Him—they don't have a choice. The earth shakes in His presence—because He is God. We, on the other hand, have a choice. We have the opportunity to go our way and do our own thing. But that would be the common thing to do. May we—*who are His beloved followers*—bend our ear toward heaven and do every single thing He tells us to do. May we hold His hand with both of ours. Read Psalm 91 again and consider His promises to us. Obedience honors Him and blesses us.

◦⊚◦

We live as one who is spoken for

Last year I wrote the book *Alone in Marriage: Encouragement for the Times When It's All Up to You*, which is a book that addresses the spiritual journey of the woman who is walking through a one-sided season in marriage. During the writing of that book, I had a recurring dream and it troubled me.

In the dream, I knew my husband; I was aware of him; we were friends, but just friends. I was dating other guys, not doing anything terrible; I was just having fun being single.

Time and time again I would run into Kevin in various places or at holiday parties. I'd smile and say, "Gee, I keep running into you!" I didn't think much of it, though. I just went on my way to the next thing on my schedule.

Toward the end of the dream, it was like a clouded lens had been taken away (that I hadn't realized was there in the first place). Suddenly in my dream I had perfect clarity, and I saw my choices to freely date other guys in the context of my actual life.

I am married to a man I deeply love. I am a mother, daughter, sister, friend, writer, speaker, and a leader in my church. I have loads of people who are counting on my obedience.

In my dream, I suddenly realized the impact of my choices, and my nerves exploded within me. I felt like shards of glass were passing through my whole body, and I was shocked and absolutely traumatized by it all. I began to hyperventilate and then woke up in a cold sweat.

I looked over at my sleeping husband and put my hand on my head. I looked around my dark bedroom, and it took me a few minutes to realize it was all just a dream. It took me hours to slow down my heart rate and to fall back asleep. I hugged my pillow, and I lay there repenting of past sins I had long since confessed, and I was absolutely shaken to my core.

This experience happened several times during the course of writing the marriage book. I decided to share my dream with a group of women I greatly trust and deeply respect. After sharing about my dream I said to them, "This book was the toughest thing I ever had to write, and I just really want to walk in the light with you all. I want you to know that I don't feel tempted to cross boundaries with other men, in any way, shape, or form. Still, I wonder if there is a trap set for me because I wrote this book on marriage."

Before I could finish my sentence a friend spoke up. "This dream has nothing to do with you and everything to do with the church."

She had my full attention.

She continued. "The way you regarded Kevin as a friend in your dream is the way so many of us have treated Jesus. We are His Bride and He is the Bridegroom, yet we've been very casual in the way we've handled our relationship with Him, sharing our affections with countless other things."

Her words left me speechless. I went home to spend a few hours with God. I opened my Bible and began to pray. I repented for every time I treated my Savior as a casual acquaintance. And I realized something. Some say, "Jesus *is* my friend; that's the kind of relationship we have." My husband is my friend too, but he is so much more than that. And for me to treat him simply as a friend is to treat him with contempt.

In my dream, I wasn't willfully sinning or stepping out on Kevin behind his back. He was just my friend. Nothing more. I really didn't know that I was doing anything wrong.

Many, many people are approaching their relationship with God and thus, their eternity, in much the same way. They go to church on Christmas and Easter, and they mention God's name on occasion. But they sincerely don't know how truly misguided they are.

"For your Maker is your husband—the Lord Almighty is his name; the Holy One of Israel is your Redeemer; he is called the God of all the earth" (Isaiah 54:5).

"If anyone is ashamed of me and my words in this adulterous and sinful generation, the Son of Man will be ashamed of him when he comes in his Father's glory with the holy angels" (Mark 8:38).

"You adulterers! Don't you realize that friendship with the world makes you an enemy of God? I say it again: If you want to be a friend of the world, you make yourself an enemy of God. What do you think the Scriptures mean when they say that the spirit God has placed within us is filled with envy? But he gives us even more grace to stand against such evil desires. As the Scriptures say, 'God opposes the proud but favors the humble'" (James 4:4–6 NLT).

God is an attentive God and He jealously longs for us, not only for our time, but also for our deepest affections. Jesus didn't lay His life down and die a torturous death just to be a sometimes friend or a casual acquaintance that we run into on holidays. He has made a covenant commitment to us. He wants intimacy.

Why are we called to such a close personal relationship with God that everything else pales in comparison? Well, because. He deserves a bride with an undivided heart. Because the moment we came to Christ, we were made new—old things passed away—and our new destiny *became a possibility*.

We were given a *legal right* to all of His treasures. We were given *instant access* to His presence and His promises (we don't have to get in line and take a number or know someone who knows someone). Our impossible call *suddenly became possible*.

We are called to oneness with God because He created us for a specific purpose. His will for us is our *best-case scenario*.

Unless we have a consistent, intimate walk with the Lord, we will never really know who we are, because we were made in His image. Unless we learn to love His presence, we will never really know what we possess in Him. Unless we consider living in His stronghold, the greatest place to be, we will never understand what it means to have all of heaven on our side. Unless our hearts beat in sync with Jesus, we will never know what kind of impact we can make in this world.

Furthermore, unless we have a consistent, intimate walk with Jesus, we will never know just how sweet and kind and true our God really is.

As the days grow more evil and the pace more frantic, only those who are intimately linked in fellowship with their Heavenly Bridegroom will actually *thrive* amidst terrifying and trying times. They are the ones who will hear His whisper; they are the ones who will have His ear; and they are the ones who will have access to every spiritual blessing in heaven.

He has chosen you. He has His heart set on you. And as you draw near to Him, He'll draw near to you. Instead of striving and hoping you'll be enough for Him, put your hope in His unfailing love, knowing it'll be more than enough for you.

When our mind-set shifts from what we must do for God to *who He is to us*, we are forever changed. It's not that we loved Him, but that He loved us. It's not how high we can jump, but that He stooped down to make us great (see Psalm 18:35; 1 John 4:10).

Truly, if we daily open ourselves up to the love God gives, we will actually be much more effective in everything we do, because our words, our prayers, and our actions will simply be a thank offering and nothing more. No more striving. No more trying to prove ourselves.

Do you want to make God smile? Do you want His heart to swell with affection for you? Put your hope in His unfailing love. Rest long in His presence. Acquire a taste for His goodness. Wrap your arms around His mercies. Trust Him enough to obey Him. Embrace big faith. Live as one who is spoken for.

In my dream the clouded lens was pulled back and I had instant clarity about the impact of my choices, and I was horrified.

One day the clouds will peel back and with a sudden and jolting clarity, the whole world will feel the impact of their choices. Some will be horrified and others will be glorified with Christ.

> *Nowhere can we get to know the holiness of God and come under its influence and power except in the inner chamber. It has been well said, "No man can expect to make progress in holiness who is not often and long alone with God."*[2]
>
> ANDREW MURRAY

Now is the time. Today is the day. No Plan B. Put your trust in Him; stay by His side; do what He says. And trust Him to provide. Expect big things, but don't *be* so big that you can't do the little things with great honor. Take time to rest in His presence, and be willing to take out a giant when He tells you to do so. Determine to give God a great return on His investment but always remember that you are not "what you do," you are someone He enjoys. First and foremost, He loves you for *you.*

Quite a thought, isn't it? You *live* in the stronghold of God and He *lives* in Your heart. To *live* from that reality is to live the uncommon life.

Beloved Bridegroom,
You are my highest desire! Awaken my heart to love You more. Take my affections and make them Yours. Keep me hidden in my vulnerable moments and set me apart when I am weak and susceptible to sin. Draw me to extended times in Your presence and pour fresh insight into my prayer life. Show me what it means to live as one who is spoken for. Heighten my conviction and strengthen my resolve to say no to the world and yes to You. You deserve all that I am and more! Thank You for loving me. I say YES to You, Lord! Amen.

Declaration:

I am blessed because I choose to live in the shelter of the Most High God. And because I live there, I can rest there. God is my refuge and my fortress; He is my God in whom I trust! He will save me from the schemes of the enemy and His faithfulness will surround me like a shield. I am my Beloved's and He is mine; His banner over me is love. I will live in such a way that the world will know that I belong to Him. The favor and the blessing, and the power of the risen Lord pours in me and through me! I make my home in the presence of the Living God. His delight is in me.

what about you?

1. Read my life verse, Psalm 116:9, and consider this. Living in the stronghold of God is not a static place. Kingdom living requires walking in His presence as we live here on earth. Describe a particular area in your life where you have a tendency to "step out of your stronghold" and thus find yourself more susceptible to attack. What can you do differently from now on? Explain.

2. Read John 14:23 and write a paraphrased prayer out of this verse. Add a request for God to help you obey in your areas of struggle.

3. Read Psalm 26:3 and break this verse down into two parts.

- How much of the day do you keep God's love ever before you, in the forefront of your mind? What can you do to increase your constant awareness of God's great love for you?

- How are you doing with walking in His truth? In other words, to what extent are you able to make your emotions submit to the truth in God's Word? Explain.

4. Read Psalm 86:11 and memorize this powerful verse. Pray it every morning. Write out this verse right now and continue writing a prayer from your heart. Come back to it again and again until you start to experience some of the things you are asking for. It's God's great delight to answer these kinds of prayers.

Expect great things from God,
attempt great things for God.[1]

WILLIAM CAREY

Now to him who is able to do immeasurably
more than all we ask or imagine, according to
his power that is at work within us, to him be
glory in the church and in Christ Jesus
throughout all generations, for ever
and ever! Amen.

EPHESIANS 3:20–21

chapter twelve

lives what
she believes

Conclusion

With all my heart I long to see women in this generation answer the call to be godly, noble, humbly dependent, holy, and confident. My heart beats faster at the thought of families, friendships, churches, and communities transforming because you took the higher road and because I took the higher road.

The ripple effect of our choice to be uncommon will start small at first, but eventually it will pick up strength and create a tidal wave of force that no gossipy, petty behavior can ever withstand.

The high road will always be higher than the low road. Mercy will always triumph over judgment. Integrity will always win out over manipulation. Humility will always trump pride. And love will always be the highest order of the day. As we walk in God's presence as we live here on earth (Psalm 116:9) we *will* establish God's Kingdom wherever we go.

Our decision to be different will surely be met with some

resistance, but with all of heaven on our side and a bit of grit on our part, we will triumph. Our skin will get a little thicker, our hearts more tender, and our priorities, well, completely rearranged; but oh, the outcome! I'm excited at the thought, aren't you?

ॐ

You, beloved and uncommon woman, are going places. Tell yourself so every single morning. Greet each new day with this bold proclamation, "I am my Beloved's and He is mine. His banner over me is love; and I am going places!" If you need a little muscle behind that statement, allow me to expound on what it means. Using the word "places" as an acronym, I want to challenge you to believe the truth about yourself, because it's perfectly wonderful and powerfully transforming.

Prized—You are His PRIZED possession. You are the apple of His eye. He is thrilled to call you His own. He loves to point you out in a crowd and whisper to the heavenly hosts, "That one right there, she is Mine. Isn't she something?"

Loved—You are LOVED. You are provided for, cherished, and covered. He died for you so you could live for Him. Each morning new mercies are waiting at your door. Each night His faithfulness covers you like a warm blanket. You are His and He is yours. His banner over you is love.

Accepted—You are ACCEPTED. You don't have to strive or pretend to be someone else. And though He wants you to be more like Him tomorrow than you are today, He accepts you just as you are right now. You are free to be real about where you are in your journey; you are free to be yourself.

Called—You are CALLED. You have such a high calling on your life that you can never accomplish even a fraction of that calling unless you stay connected to the Vine and believe with all your heart that you are anointed, appointed, and called to change your world. God has a wonderful assignment for you.

Equipped—You are EQUIPPED. You could never exhaust all of the resources made available to you in Christ Jesus. He has made all grace abound to you so that you can abound in every single thing He's called you to accomplish. Where He calls, He equips. You have everything you need and more.

Sent—You are SENT. You are comforted in your trials that you might be a comforter. You are given courage in trying times that you might be an encourager. You are made rich in every way that you might be generous on every occasion. You have things to do. You are sent. How will you know where to go? Let His peace be your guide.

‿◉◞

Here's a gentle reminder. *The call to change the world begs us to do* something *to help the poor and the oppressed.*

Isaiah 58:10–11 says, "If you feed those who are hungry and take care of the needs of those who are troubled, then your light will shine in the darkness, and you will be bright like sunshine at noon. The Lord will always lead you. He will satisfy your needs in dry lands and give strength to your bones. You will be like a garden that has much water, like a spring that never runs dry" (NCV).

When a friend, who was raised as a missionary kid in Africa, traveled to America, she asked this question, "Mommy, did God run out of money halfway around the world?" We must, as abundantly provided-for children of God, use some of our resources to help the destitute.

But this is not a call to carry the world's load on our shoulders . . .

Jesus said, "Take my yoke upon you and learn from me, for I am gentle and humble in heart, and you will find rest for your souls. For my yoke is easy and my burden is light" (Matthew 11:29–30).

You've heard the song "He's got the whole world, in His hands." *He's* carrying the whole world; we just need to carry what He has given to us. He's the One who put the stars in place. He's the One who spoke the world into being. He's the One who flooded the earth and then promised not to do it again. He longs for us to hear His whisper, *I know you and how transient you are. I know what makes you weak and I know what makes you smile. Trust Me in this. I've fashioned for you a life assignment that fits you perfectly. It's not too heavy for you but it's weighty enough to strengthen you. Develop your gifts, care for the least and the lost, and love Me first. This is the powerful life.*

Some women are so overwhelmed by all of the wrongs in their world that they refuse to take on *any* of the burden. Instead they construct a comfortable, safe, and small existence; and as a result, they slowly lose touch with the realities of the very people Jesus asked us to care for.

Other women are so immersed in what's wrong that they see little right with the world. They are mad that others aren't doing more, and their lives are marked by more stress than joy.

We are called to neither of these extremes.

Though it may be tempting to pursue the American dream and turn a deaf ear to the suffering and the lost, we cannot and must not. Though the world's suffering could crush us, we must not let it because we'll be no good to anyone buried under a heap of helplessness.

Carefully planted in our souls is a conviction to right *some* of the wrongs in our day. Our Kingdom concern may only be in seed form right now, but it was purposefully placed there for us to nurture and cultivate.

How do we find out which portion of God's giant burden *we* are supposed to carry? We spend extended amounts of time with our Savior. We listen to His voice. We expose ourselves to the different needs around us and we offer some assistance. We send money to ministries helping the poor and the sick. We go on mission trips. We donate some time at the local food shelf.

Eventually we will stumble upon several causes that we are meant to became engaged with. It might be the AIDS epidemic in Africa; it might be the issue of human trafficking or of life for the unborn. It might be the issue of hunger, or inner-city children who need a mentor.

Prayerfully "watch" Jesus as you read the New Testament. You'll find Him with the hungry, the sick, and the marginalized. When you help them, you help Him, and He will repay you (see Proverbs 19:17; Matthew 25:40). We don't have to do it all. That would be impossible. But we are called to do *something*.

☙

You have a gift made just for you. It is wrapped in a beautiful package with a lovely bow. It is a robe of righteousness. This gift allows you to stand before God and to participate in His divine nature. You must always remember that you are a woman of extreme worth. You are royalty.

On the days when the world tries to dress you with labels and assessments that are inconsistent with heaven's voice, tighten your belt and speak the truth: "I cannot wear *those* rags with *this* robe . . . they do not go together, and I choose righteousness." This choice will change your day; it will change your life.

You've had a bath— you are clean because you have accepted Christ's sacrifice for your sins. Now let Him wash your feet—on a regular basis. Don't ever fool yourself into thinking that since everyone else has dirty feet that your grime doesn't matter, because it does. It matters because you were created for a holy purpose. Believe this and live by it.

You are a masterpiece created for a beautiful purpose. Don't let the sin of this world weigh you down. This world is changed daily because you are a part of it. Keep your robe of righteousness on, keep your feet clean, and determine to pursue the high calling of a godly life.

After all He has done for us, does anything seem more important than living a life that pleases Him?

I agree. Nothing else compares.

May the Lord God, the Holy One of Israel, bless you and make you a blessing. May His face shine upon you as you determine to live a life that is pleasing to Him. May you never settle for halfhearted living since you've been offered continual abundance. May you never be content to shuffle on the low road when our Savior has called you to the higher way. May you always be filled to the fullness of God until you reach the other side. May you now, with all of the faith you can muster, receive and appropriate the gifts God has given you. I pray you will speak and live with holy confidence and humble dependence. May you determine to live a life of radical love and powerful servanthood. May your life reflect the true meaning of living as an uncommon woman.

> When he had finished washing their feet, he put on his clothes and returned to his place. "Do you understand what I have done for you?" he asked them. "You call me 'Teacher' and 'Lord,' and rightly so, for that is what I am. Now that I, your Lord and Teacher, have washed your feet, you also should wash one another's feet. I have set you an example that you should do as I have done for you." (John 13:12–15)

notes

Before We Begin

1. *Oxford American Writer's Thesaurus*, compiled by Christine A. Lindberg (Oxford Univ. Press, 2004) s.v. "uncommon."

Chapter One: *Humbly Accepts Acceptance*

1. Brennan Manning, *Ruthless Trust* (New York: Harper Collins, 2000), 30.
2. "Accept Acceptance" phrase borrowed from author Paul Tillich, *The Shaking of Foundations* (New York: Charles Scribner's Sons, 1948), 42.
3. Graham Cooke, *The Language of Love* (Grand Rapids: Chosen Books, 2004), 47.
4. Brennan Manning, *The Ragamuffin Gospel* (Sisters, Ore.: Multnomah), 54.
5. Martin Luther, Quotemeal from Heartlight (heartlight.org).
6. Greek from the NAS New Testament Greek Lexicon on Crosswalk.com.

Chapter Two: *Gets Back Up Again*

1. Bob Sorge, *Secrets of the Secret Place* (Greenwood, Mo.: Oasis House, 2001), 62.
2. Attributed to Morris at www.bearersoflight.org/Jan05BOLM.pdf.

Chapter Three: *Wisely Chooses Her Battles*

1. Rick Renner, *Sparkling Gems from the Greek* (Tulsa, Okla.: Teach All Nations, 2003), 229.
2. A. W. Tozer, *The Pursuit of God* (Camp Hill, Penn.: Christian Publications, 1995), 179–180.
3. "Beloved Enemies" is a term originated by LeeAnn Payne.
4. Brennan Manning, *The Ragamuffin Gospel* (Sisters, Ore.: Mult-nomah), 146–147.

Chapter Four: *Forgives, Receives, Stands, Bows, and Believes*

1. Quin Sherrer and Ruthanne Garlock, *The Making of a Spiritual Warrior* (Ann Arbor, Mich.: Servant, 1998), 23.
2. "Un-offendable" phrase from Francis Frangipane, "In Christ's Image Training," 2002, Arrow Publications, Cedar Rapids, Iowa, Level 1, CD #6.
3. Brian Simmons, *Song of Songs: Journey of the Bride* (Tulsa: Insight Publishing, 2002), 35.
4. http://bible.crosswalk.com/Lexicons/Hebrew/heb.cgi?number=04929&version=kjv.
5. Andrew Murray, *Humility* (Minneapolis: Bethany, 2001), Luther quote referenced on 43.
6. J. Oswald Sanders, *Spiritual Leadership* (Chicago: Moody, 1967, 1980, 1994), 52.

Chapter Five: *Understands that Love Sees and Love Covers*

1. Michael Youssef, *The Spirituality That Heals* (Colorado Springs: Waterbrook, 2003), 56.
2. This paragraph was written by my friend Sandy Forsberg
3. C. S. Lewis, *C. S. Lewis, Readings for Meditation and Reflection* (New York: Harper Collins, 1992), 62.

Chapter Six: *Values Truth Over Perception*

1. This paragraph was written by my friend Sandy Forsberg.
2. Graham Cooke, *God Revealed* (Grand Rapids: Chosen Books, 2003, 2005), 56.
3. Ibid., 52.

Chapter Seven: *Chooses Mercy Over Judgment*

1. A. W. Tozer , *The Knowledge of the Holy* (New York: Harper & Row, 1961), 90.

2. I wrote this imaginative portrayal of the adulterous woman based on the book of John, chapter 8.
3. Tozer, 91.
4. *Oxford American Writer's Thesaurus*, compiled by Christine A. Lindberg (Oxford Univ. Press, 2004), s.v. "judge."
5. Ibid., s.v. "mercy."

Chapter Eight: *Chooses Prayer Over Pettiness*

1. E. M. Bounds quote from prayer flip calendar, "On My Knees" (Bloomington, Minn.: Garborgs, 2000), September 17th entry.
2. Gene Edwards, *A Tale of Three Kings* (Wheaton, Ill.: Tyndale, 1980, 1992), 33–35.
3. Friend, Pastor Jim Olson; Mentor, Bob Mumford.
4. A. W. Tozer , *The Knowledge of the Holy* (New York: Harper & Row, 1961), 57.
5. O. Hallesby quote from prayer flip calendar, "On My Knees" (Bloomington, Minn.: Garborgs, 2000), October 23rd entry.

Chapter Nine: *Will Not Be Bullied by Her Fears*

1. Joyce Meyer, *Never Lose Heart*, (Tulsa: Harrison House, 2001), 113.
2. Susie Larson, *Alone in Marriage* (Chicago: Moody, 2007), 55.
3. Quin Sherrer and Ruthanne Garlock, *The Making of a Spiritual Warrior* (Ann Arbor, Mich.:, Servant, 1998), 93.
4. Rick Renner, *Sparkling Gems from the Greek* (Tulsa, Okla.: Teach all Nations, 2003), 629.
5. Hannah Hurnard, *Hinds' Feet on High Places* (Wheaton, Ill.: Tyndale, 1975), 125–127.
6. A.W. Tozer, *The Pursuit of God* (Camp Hill, Penn.: Christian Publications, 1995), 95.

Chapter Ten: *Believes His Promises Are True*

1. A.W. Tozer, *The Pursuit of God* (Camp Hill, Penn.: Christian Publications, 1995), 71.
2. Oswald Chambers, *My Utmost for His Highest* (Grand Rapids, Mich.: Discovery House, 1935, 1995), May 9th entry.
3. Graham Cooke, *Drawing Close* (Grand Rapids, Mich.: Chosen Books, 2003, 2005), 48.

Chapter Eleven: *Stays in the Stronghold of God*

1. Francis Frangipane, *The Stronghold of God* (Lake Mary, Fla.: Charisma House, 1994, 1998), 6.
2. Andrew Murray, *Humility* (Minneapolis: Bethany, 2001), 95.

Chapter Twelve: *Lives What She Believes*

1. Mary Tileston, *Joy & Strength* (New York: Barnes & Noble, 1993), 262.

ENCOURAGEMENT FOR THE TIMES
WHEN IT'S ALL UP TO YOU

Alone in Marriage

SUSIE LARSON

ISBN-10: 0-8024-5278-7
ISBN-13: 978-0-8024-5278-8

Books abound for those whose marriages are crumbling or have ended. But what about those marriages committed "til death do us part" and yet are going through a period of time when one spouse is carrying the burden? What happens to a woman when marriage gets heavy and she gets weary? Often, when a woman ends up carrying the weight of the marriage (due to her husband's health, choices, workload, etc.), her tendency is to "get out or check out."

She may consider her husband's distraction an opportunity to do her own thing. But is there a better way to walk through this season? Even thrive? Susie Larson stands in as an encouraging friend, walking with you, helping you to discern how anxiety and anger will slow you down; and how loneliness and disappointment can actually refine and bless you. You will be challenged and inspired as you wrap your arms around this time and remember that God has His arms around you.

by Susie Larson
Find it now at your favorite local or online bookstore.

www.MoodyPublishers.com